Malaysian Food

Cameron Highlands, Malaysia.

Malaysian Food

*A collection of my favourite dishes
and the inspiration behind them*

Norman Musa

In memory of my late Mum & Dad.
Words cannot describe how
grateful I am... thank you.

First published in Great Britain in 2009
This International Edition first published as the Malaysian Edition in 2010
Reprinted (with minor amendments) in 2011 by

Ning Limited
92-94 Oldham Street
Northern Quarter
Manchester
M4 1LJ
United Kingdom

www.ningcatering.com

Edited by Andy Spracklen
Book design and setting by Colin Hall
Ning logo design by Yosrie Yunos
Photography by Ben Page, Adam Ong and Norman Musa
Marketing and PR by Victoria Watson and Nori Anwar
Assistant Chef Ling Ling Tong
Food styling by Norman Musa and Giulia Zonza
Ning wallpaper design by The Art Surgery, Manchester

ISBN 978-0-9563772-1-0

Printed and bound in Singapore

Contents

*The recipes in this book are intended for a
Western taste palette. Please feel free to add
more chillies to your cooking if you wish.*

Norman Musa

A Malaysian Northerner in Northern England

Born and brought up in Butterworth, Penang, Norman Musa is the creator, co-owner and Executive Chef of Ning restaurant in Manchester in the North West of England, UK.

A *kampung* boy by upbringing, he came to the UK in 1994 to train as a quantity surveyor at the University of Portsmouth. It was as a student that, despite his family's restaurant and food stall business, he discovered that he did not know how to cook! Being a resourceful, tenacious sort, he was soon in regular touch with his late Mum who mentored him over the phone and when back home in Malaysia in the art of fabulous home cooking.

Working as a Quantity Surveyor first in Bournemouth and then London, he would regularly cook and host family-like feasts for all his Malaysian friends and their friends in the UK. They and his now business partner, Andy, observed the skill, passion and dedication by which he would not just expertly cook but creatively present his amazing food at such parties.

With such a passion for his native food and having been mentored in his cooking skills by his Mum, he and his friends started to dream about running a restaurant which would showcase the wonderful food that he grew up with. But it was not until 2003 when Norman moved to Manchester that the dream became a reality. With the city centre changing fast with new apartments and urban dwellers, Manchester seemed to be a ripe for something new and different.

Ning restaurant was finally born in 2006 and since then Norman has shaped it into a critically acclaimed restaurant, which was nominated for Restaurant of the Year in 2009.

In 2007 Chef Norman launched his Malaysian cookery classes, which has given him the opportunity to promote Malaysian food to the locals and which have since proven phenomenally popular. Teaching his students how to cook classic dishes like *Rendang, Gulai* and *Murtabak,* he has also demonstrated Malaysian cooking at city food festivals and on TV.

Norman and Ning restaurant have appeared in well-known UK publications including *The Sunday Times, The Daily Telegraph, The Guardian* and *Time Out,* and in Malaysia in *The Star* and on TV3, TV9 and Astro, including on *In Person, Awani Pagi* and *Nasi Lemak Kopi O.* His first TV appearance in the UK was on Market Kitchen with celebrity chefs Rachel Allen, Mark Sargeant and Matt Tebbutt.

Norman's ambition is to be a global ambassador for Malaysian cuisine. His goal is already on the way to being realised in 2010 with his appointment as Race Chef for the *Lotus Racing* Formula One team. A prestigious opportunity, Norman will be the only Malaysian chef at each race around the world, serving both crews and VIP's.

His style and approach is unique. Characterised by colour, simplicity, freshness, quality and style – just like this book – Chef Norman's recipes are easy to follow and adapted to Western and global tastes that will help Malaysian food, the unsung hero of South East Asian cuisine, to be 'the next big thing'.

Chef Norman's recent TV appearances in Malaysia and the UK

Contemporary approach founded on traditional culture

Perhaps Norman's most significant achievement at Ning restaurant has been his ability to carefully balance authenticity with contemporary touches. For a Western audience at least, this has been an important factor in his and Ning's success to date.

Whilst in the UK, Norman has developed his interest in traditional Malay culture and its culinary arts. Prior to opening the restaurant, he performed at cultural festivals in the UK with a South East Asian performing arts group, *Nusantara*, including to an audience of HM Queen Elizabeth II.

His restaurant's theme, and its name, symbolises the integrated nature of Malay cooking with its traditional and unique cultural practices. The name 'Ning' itself derives from a musical note used in traditional Malay music known as *gamelan*. The *gamelan* instrumentalists wear *songket*, either in the form of the *sampin* (skirt-like adornment), *bengkung* (waistband) or *tanjak* (headgear). Together with *kerawang* (lace-like embroidery) and *bunga lawang*, these motifs decorate parts of Ning restaurant.

The *songket* is a typically Asian woven cloth, using gold coloured or silver thread and with designs inspired by insightful observations of nature. It is often highly imaginative and tends to include scenes of animals, birds, flowers, trees and especially spices. The figures of clove (*cengkih*) and star anise (*bunga lawang*) recur frequently in *songket* design. When integrated into the *songket*, normally the *bunga lawang* comprises an eight point star in a four-cornered weave. This motif has been used for more than 200 years.

Star anise, in particular, is a pretty-looking, fresh and aromatic spice and one of the most important ingredients in Asian recipes, such as curries and soups. But Chef Norman has a more important reason for including the *bunga lawang* as a decorative motif in his restaurant. It reminds him of his late mother, whose recipes often made use of the same spice and which went on to inspire his own cooking. The *bunga lawang* motifs thus take pride of place in his personalised *songket*.

Loseng benangnya halus sentuhan,	The silk thread spun so soft and fine,
Tekun si hawa membuat tenunan,	When the hand of Eve did make the weave,
Songket indahya seni warisan,	May the craft of *songket* never decline,
Tetap bernilai zaman berzaman.	So its beauty will stay and never leave.
Anak dara duduk sekawan,	Together sit the pretty young maidens,
Anggun berselendang nampak sopan,	Adorned with scarves all looking demure,
Songket Terengganu berbunga lawang,	Woven *songket* with *bunga lawang* as patterns,
Memikat hati indah gemerlapan.	Capture your heart with shining allure.
Kalau tuan ke Tanjung Senu,	If you go to *Tanjung Senu*,
Pulangkan hamba si ikan emas	A goldfish I ask that you bring,
Indah sungguh songket Terengganu,	So stunning the *songket* of *Terengganu*,
Bunga lawang berbenangkan emas.	With *bunga lawang* blooms of golden string.

We wish Chef Norman all the best in his continuing efforts to raise the appreciation of the amazing traditional Malay culture in popular

abroad when cooking for friends and family at home. So many people come into my restaurant as a result of spending time travelling in the Far East and there is no greater compliment than when someone recognises the authenticity of the food we serve at Ning.

My aim in running Ning and the cookery classes has always been to try to re-create the passion and culture surrounding Malaysian food. Food brings Malaysians together. It is the foundation of our social activity and we will travel far and at any time of the day in search of good food. My passion for cooking comes naturally and I believe it runs in my blood. My brother is also a chef and my sister has recently started a cake business so it's definitely a family thing. Despite my love of food and cooking I never thought I would open my own restaurant, but having seen my parents run their own, inspired me to take on the challenge to open Ning.

Most of the recipes in this book I inherited from my Mum who was the best cook I have ever known. Every meal she cooked went without complaint, apart from me pointing out how oily it was sometimes. It's only since I moved to the UK that I have become more conscious of eating healthily.

Her major influence lives on in the cooking I do both at home and in the Ning kitchen.

About
Malaysian
Food

Malaysian food, the unsung cuisine at the heart of South East Asia, is in fact rich in flavour and diversity. If you're passionate about food, you will not be able to help yourself becoming passionate about Malaysian food.

Like its nation, Malaysian cuisine reflects the intricate tapestry of culture, heritage, geography and trade that fuses the culinary traditions and flavours of Asian, Arabian and European cooking. Covering a full spectrum of cuisine from Portuguese, Arab and Indian to Chinese, Thai and Indonesian, Malaysian food is a fascinating journey of all that is 'truly Asia' in one nation.

Unlike many modern Western lifestyles, food remains at the very heart of Malaysian society and family life. Big cook-up banquets for family gatherings, eating out daily at friendly local hawker stalls and roadside restaurants, or cooking for 2,000 wedding guests are all part of the cultural scene. What's more eating is a 24/7 activity, and it's certainly not unheard of eating out at 2am, with the whole family in tow.

Although the big supermarket chains, including that British one with the red and blue logo, now have a presence in many towns and cities, thankfully the vibrancy of traditional street life remains alive in many areas like Penang and it is here that you experience the authentic vibe and taste of Malaysian cooking.

Much of the food cycle is relatively sustainable, with a vibrant informal economy of small producers and fresh regional produce. Again, diversity is strong in the wonderful array of fruits and vegetables that generate a vivid kaleidoscope of colour in the village markets and on the city streets.

Like many other South East Asian countries, traditional Malaysian food culture is a full-on sensory experience; one that I have grown up with and one that I want to share.

So in this, my first book, I introduce Malaysian cooking – particularly ethnic Malay cuisine, which is my heritage – and the secrets of my cooking from home classics to my own fusion creations.

The story behind Malaysian food

To really understand Malaysian cuisine, it is essential to appreciate its layers of history that have woven the tapestry of Malaysian culture as found today.

Malaysia forms part of South East Asia – also comprising the nations of Thailand, Myanmar (Burma), Cambodia, Laos, Vietnam, Philippines, Indonesia, Brunei, Singapore, Timor-Leste (East Timor) and Papua New Guinea – and sits on two land masses: Malaysian Borneo (often referred to as East Malaysia) and the mainland, Peninsular Malaysia (sometimes known as West Malaysia). Formed of three federal territories and 13 states, two of which – Sabah and Sarawak – form East Malaysia, the country is relatively young having achieved independence from the British just over 50 years ago in 1957.

Unique in the world, Malaysia has a rotating monarchy whereby the Sultans of nine States take it in turn to be King, Supreme Head of State. Therefore, typically Malaysian, every 5 years there is a day off to celebrate the coronation. Given annual celebrations of all the major faiths and cultures – Eid al-Fitr, Christmas, Diwali, Chinese New Year, *Hari Merdeka* (Independence Day) and others – there is plenty of time off to feast with friends and family throughout the year.

It is the geography of Malaysia that has lent itself to the rich tapestry of cultures – especially food culture – that exists today.

Malaysia is strategically located at the heart of the region where the vast oceans of the Indian and Pacific embrace each other. Coupled with the prevailing winds and ocean currents, it was also a natural trading post for ships from Arabia and Eurasia. By the 14th century AD it was the south west city of *Melaka* (Malacca) that had established itself as the most significant trading port in the entire region. Thanks to its geographic position and its progressively-minded Sultans, *Melaka* became a bustling magnet for Arab and Chinese traders in particular. Bringing their textiles, earthenware, spices and philosophies with them, the Strait of Malacca became a strategic trading channel for the region and beyond. The conversion of one Sultan to Islam by Arab traders brought the propagation of the faith to this part of world, whilst the exciting array of valuable aromatic spices brought about new adventures in food culture that influence the flavours of Malaysia today.

Come the 16th century, the Europeans began to appreciate the amazing delights of this part of the world. It was the intrepid and entrepreneurial Portuguese that first discovered the economic powerhouse of *Melaka* and the trade rewards that could be garnered. Attempting to establish a rival port, Singapore, they soon discovered that *Melaka* could not be outdone and so utilised their military advancements to launch an assault on the city.

With their success (cutting a long story short, of course), the first colonists in the region soon brought their own innovations in food culture. Known for their use of ingredients like vinegar, pickles, shallots, limes, tamarind and other sour fruits, the Portuguese influenced Malaysian food like no other subsequent colonist did. But it was the icon of South East Asian cooking – the chilli – that was the greatest legacy of the southern Europeans. Now synonymous with the region's cooking, the chilli in fact originates from the Americas. With a local palette of 'heat' in food through the use of fresh peppercorns and being on the same latitude as the Portuguese's South American colonies, they soon cottoned on to South East Asia's vast potential for the chilli.

One Sultan of *Melaka* is famous for marrying Chinese princess Hang Li Po who, whilst taking on many of the local Malay customs and dress, maintained much of her culinary heritage. The resultant Chinese-Malay fusion with undertones of Portuguese influences led to what is known as *Nyonya* cuisine, the epitome of what many even today refer to as the 'melting pot' of Malaysian culture.

The 18th and 19th centuries saw the dominance of Dutch and British trade and rule in the region; the Dutch eventually colonising Indonesia while the British Malaya, as they called it. With them, the British brought in Chinese workers to labour in the tin mines and Indian workers in the rubber plantations – which even today remains Malaysia's No.1 export. This mix of peoples further diversified the communities of Malaysia leading to the present where approximately 60% are Malays, officially Muslim; 20% Chinese, many of whom are Christian, Buddhist or of Chinese belief; and 8% Indian, mostly Hindu or Muslim. The remaining 12% are of other Asian, Borneo tribal extraction or Caucasian ex-patriots.

As a result Malaysia is a truly multi-cultural, multi-faith society carefully managed through successive governments' visions of what it is to be Malaysian, rather than just Malay.

It is this so-called melting pot of cultures that is reflected in the incredible variety of cuisine – from the freshest exotic seafood and robust, coconut-laced Malay curries to the aromatic spices, rich gravies and sensational breads (*roti*) of Indian cuisine to the Chinese-style fragrant soups and wok-fried noodles..

The spectrum of Malaysian food

Malaysian food can best be imagined as a spectrum of various pedigree and hybrid cuisines. Malay cuisine, at the centre as it were, is characterised by robust, flavoursome 'wet' and 'dry' curries with key ingredients being coconut milk, lemongrass, chilli, onion, ginger, galangal, lime leaves, turmeric, sugar, salt and of course various spices.

Classic Malay dishes include the popular dish *Nasi Lemak* – a delightful combination of coconut milk and spice-infused rice served with chilli *sambal* (like a paste), cucumber, peanuts, hardboiled egg and fabulous crispy dried anchovies – the core ingredients of which are traditionally wrapped up in banana leaves. Another signature dish is the rich, coconutty dry curry *Rendang* which combines much of those traditional core Malay ingredients into a exquisite, melt-in-the-mouth meat stew that is particularly popular at weddings or when celebrating the Muslim festival of Eid al-Fitr.

Indian Muslim food is focused on curries of rich spicy gravies and *roti* such as my favourite *Roti Canai* – a delicious buttery bread

that having had its dough theatrically stretched and thrown about is then puffed into a square on to a hot plate, slightly char cooked, resulting in a very popular flaky flatbread that is torn and dipped into various curry and vegetable dahl sauces, typically for breakfast. Another hallmark of Indian Muslim cuisine is fish head curry – yes, the heads of fish complete with their eyeballs are simmered in an aromatic spicy 'gravy' until all the fish juices, that are at their best in the head, ooze into a brilliantly tasty dish worth overcoming your nervousness for.

Indian spices are paramount here – cardamon, fennel, coriander seeds, cinnamon, chilli powder and fenugreek – and leaves such as mint, coriander and curry. Flavours are rich, complex and spicy.

Often referred to as *Mamak* food, Indian Muslim food is well-represented in Malaysian street food at popular 24/7 *Mamak* stalls run by Tamil Muslims whose forefathers migrated to Malaysia from South India; favourite dishes of which are *Murtabak*, which I teach in my Cookery School, and *Rojak*. *Murtabak* is essentially a chunky omelette, typically with shredded chicken, onions, spices, turmeric and chilli, that is encased in a simple, thin, pancake-like pastry (see p75). I prefer to make mine crispy. It's often served with a curry dip and makes for a filling snack at any time of the day. *Rojak* meanwhile is a medley of warm vegetables, roots and egg, sometimes with strips of calamari (squid) or chicken, and laced with a sweet and spicy chilli or peanut sauce.

Indian Muslim and Malay food is always 'halal' – which forbids the use of pork and alcohol and for which permitted animal ingredients have been slaughtered to Muslim rituals. Indian Hindu cuisine tends to be rich in vegetarian cuisine and additionally excludes the use of beef. Chinese cuisine however is generally not halal, frequently using pork and other forbidden ingredients for Muslims. This means, I have to admit, that I rarely visit Chinese stalls and restaurants when back home in Malaysia. It also means that my experience of Chinese cuisine in Malaysia is more in the Malay style – classics like *Char Kuey Teow*, Hainanese Chicken Rice and Curry Mee – all of which you will easily find on the streets of towns like my hometown Penang.

Most Chinese Malaysian food is relatively less spicy than most other styles on the food spectrum. However, we Malaysians have made it our own, adding spicier touches to it. *Char Kuey Teow*, for example, is a very popular fried noodle dish made with wide flat rice noodles, wok fried with vegetables such as beansprouts, soy sauce, meat and traditionally cockles – but with an added kick of chilli paste. My favourite, Hainanese Chicken Rice or *Nasi Ayam* is a medley-style dish like *Nasi Lemak* comprising poached or deep-fried chicken (yes, Malaysians do love their chicken!) typically on the bone with chicken stock-infused rice and chicken stock-based vegetable soup on the side (Malaysians don't throw away food like many Westerners do) – but the real kick is in the amazing chilli, ginger, garlic and lime paste to accompany it.

Mohd Shukur, 'Super Roti Man', preparing *Roti Canai*.

The Malaysian Market

I love going to Malaysian markets because the ingredients are so colourful and fresh. So fresh in fact that you can almost feel and smell the freshness as you walk in. Not like sterile supermarkets, which I hope don't take over Malaysia like in the UK.

As with so much of my cooking experience, my Mum taught me everything there is to know about freshness and picking the very best ingredients – and she was an expert at bartering!

We used to spend a good three hours in the market buying all the fresh ingredients to cook lunch. Well, that included breaks for breakfast and the time my Mum spent telling me all the latest local gossip and catching up with her friends who we bumped into along the way.

Before we would leave the house, she would have decided what to cook for lunch. What always amazed me is that my Mum would not write down the ingredients she needed to buy. Instead she would memorise them. My Dad meanwhile was like a chauffeur, driving us to all the shops we needed to visit. Her favourite market was the *Kepala Batas* market near Butterworth (Penang).

You can get everything there – wet and dry ingredients – from colourful fruit and vegetables, exotic fish and whole meats to hand mixed spices, freshly squeezed coconut milk, salted fish, dried anchovies, and homemade curry sauces. Just writing about it, makes me want to be there.

When back home, I tend to get up early to go to the market at around 7.30am, a busy time on the roads as school children and workers make their way to their schools, offices and factories. Getting there early though is essential to get the freshest possible ingredients and to avoid the crowds at the market.

When I was younger I always took the opportunity to ask my Mum about the ingredients as we browsed and she would explain to me patiently (while my Dad waited patiently in the car). Now of course I know everything – from lemongrass to ginger flower!

Fishmonger filleting stingray.

When I get to the market, I always head first to the seafood area where there are about 10 fishmonger stalls all selling fantastic freshly caught seafood – most of which is from *Kuala Muda* fishing village, about 40km away on the west coast. There is an amazing variety of fish available, sometimes including shark and sting ray. My favourites though are Black Pomfret which has a light texture and sweet, rich flavour, and Sea Catfish with a wonderful delicate flesh, finer than Sea Bass. Prawns, calamari, crabs, clams, mussels and cockles abound too, all piled high on the stalls competing for my attention.

There is also freshwater fish such as Freshwater Catfish, Tilapia and freshwater prawns – none of which are my favourites because they have a strong earthier smell. For me, Sea Catfish is perfect for a really good fish curry.

I normally browse three or four stalls before deciding which stall to get the fish from. It's all about freshness. You can tell by looking at the fish eyes whether the fish are fresh or not. If the eyes have gone red, then the fish are not fresh; simple as that. I often pinch the fish too to check whether the flesh is firm or soft. If firm then the fish is fresh.

Next to the fish stalls are the meat stalls selling chicken, beef, goat and sometimes buffalo meat – all halal, of course. There are two types of chicken – *ayam kampung* (literally 'village chicken') is organic chicken which is smaller and more expensive but local and with a richer flavour – or farmed chicken. I normally get the best chicken from Zaitun, a lovely bubbly happy lady who runs her own stall. We use the whole chicken, so I normally buy a whole or half of one from her depending on what and how much I am cooking.

Having got the meat and fish, it's time for the vegetable stalls. All colourfully laid out on the floor or tables, you can tell they are freshly picked by the aromas and the sight of soil on the vegetables. The cucumbers are so crisp and crunchy. Greens like water spinach, used a lot in Chinese cooking, are bunched up with rubber bands – no plastic wrapping like supermarkets; Malaysian markets get all your

senses going. And then there are turmeric leaves, kaffir lime leaves, curry leaves; tomatoes, chillies, aubergines; and okra which I also buy for my fish curry. So much; so fresh.

Then there is a fantastic stall selling fresh coconut milk. Something that I wish I could get more easily in the UK. You can see how they chop the coconut open and take the white flesh from the hard shell. Then grate the flesh, using a special device we call *kukur kelapa*, and hand-squeeze the grated coconut to extract the milk. These days guys like Hanif and Munir use a machine to do this but 20 years ago I can remember everything was done by hand.

Heading to the dry ingredients area – beginning to think of my breakfast by now – you can find dried fish like anchovies piled high in sacks, bottled sauces like soy all lined up decoratively on shelves, fresh shrimp paste in slabs, ready-made sauces in Tupperware containers... I could go on. I always get my anchovies from Fatimah, a gregarious stall owner. I remember a few years back she used to run the stall on her own but, every year I go home, her stall gets bigger with new staff – she must be doing something right!

After all that shopping, and with my hands beginning to be full of carrying bags, it is time for a break. I always buy my favourite *roti canai* from 'Super Roti Man', Mohd Shukur, the winner of many regional and national competitions. His *roti* is the best. When I was with my Mum, she would always get *Nasi Lemak*, Malaysia's national dish of coconut rice (see page 140) served with boiled egg, peanuts, crispy dried anchovies, cucumber, chilli *sambal* paste and sometimes chicken or fish. While I eat, the street cats roam around vying for attention and scraps of food. I wash it down with a strong but sweet Malaysian tea, *teh tarik* (see p164), giving me the energy to do yet more shopping.

For the curries, we need spices of course. While Malaysians often cheat and buy the ready-made packets of curry powders, it is Fairoz Khan's stall that is the best. He still sells the spices individually by

Hanif, the coconut milk man.

hand. I just tell what I'm cooking and he mixes up what I need for, say, a fish curry.

Finally, it's back to the main hall of the market with all the fresh fruit and vegetables. So many stalls scattered across the floor, with all the local produce arranged neatly in plastic baskets or in colourful piles. Dried and fresh chillies, *petai* (known as stink or bitter bean, a healthy green type of bean in a twisted pod), big bunches of spinach and other leaves and fresh fruits like *rambutan*, lychee, *mangosteen* – all so fragrant with pale juicy flesh within their respective hairy, rough and smooth husks – dragon fruit, jackfruit and mangoes. At the village home, we used to have trees in the garden growing most of these when I was young.

But it is the notorious *durian* that is considered to be the king of fruits that is the finale of my visit to the market – it's curious, love or hate, sweet and savoury aroma and taste is so pungent that it is banned in most hotels and on airlines. Eaten hot or cold, on its own or in a curry or dessert, it is a spiky and heavy melon-shaped fruit that you know you have eaten up to three days later! My parents used to fill the boot of the car with them, whereas most Westerners do not like *durian*. So I always dare my Cookery School students to try it.

Malaysian faces.

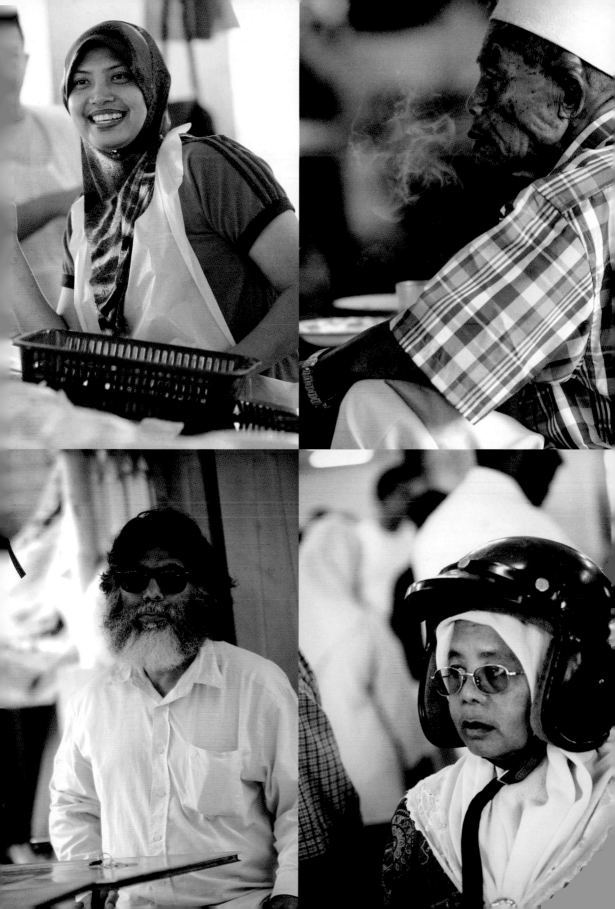

Norman's family faces.

Malaysian faces.

Essential
Ingredients

The exciting thing about Malaysian cooking is all the ingredients and their flavours and aromas.

However, some of the ingredients used are less well-known to many people in the UK. So I thought I would illustrate them – and also recommend a few brands that, in my opinion, are superior.

In most British cities like Manchester and London you can pick up the ingredients in specialist oriental and South Asian grocery stores, and increasingly in the 'world foods' aisles of major supermarkets. In Malaysia, of course, you can find these ingredients much more easily.

You might wonder why I blend many of the more familiar ingredients like garlic, ginger and onion. This is because the blended ingredients mix well with the sauces, resulting in a richer flavour. For cooking oil, I use vegetable oil, but you can also use corn or sunflower. The strong flavour of olive oil, however, is not suitable as it will be overpowering.

My food is for any occasion – not just at dinner parties. So most of the recipes are designed for serving two people. Simply adjust proportionately to suit your occasion. And if you like your food very spicy, just add more chillies.

Lengkuas
Galangal

This herb is of the same family as ginger. The aroma and flavour is very pungent and citrusy. You only need to use a bit in a recipe otherwise the dish will turn slightly bitter. 100g of fresh galangal peeled and blended with 100ml of water can produce up to 10 tablespoons paste. In the UK you find it in the chiller cabinet of oriental grocery stores.

Serai
Lemongrass

This is one of my favourite herbs. The refreshing fragrance makes recipes smell so fresh and aromatic. 4 stalks of lemongrass blended with 150ml water can give up to 10 tablespoons paste. Having cut off the tip, use the bottom half of a lemongrass stalk, chopping it into small pieces before blending it with the water. When frying it, it is best to extract the juice from the pulp so the oil will not spit.

Cili Kering
Dried Chilli Paste

Dried chillies are used a lot in Malaysian cooking. The colour is a rich, gorgeous crimson compared to using fresh chillies, and the flavour sweeter and more intense than sharp. 20 dried chillies (the bigger the better) with 150ml of water can give up to 10 tablespoons of chilli paste. To prepare, bring to the boil 1 litre of water and boil the dried chillies for 10 minutes. Remove the chilli stalk beforehand if there is any. Drain the water and blend the chillies with 150ml cold water in a blender. You can always soak the chillies overnight to soften the chillies first.

Daun Kari
Curry Leaves

Curry leaves originate from India, and consequently are a typical ingredient in Indian style Malaysian dishes. Buying fresh ones is best. In the UK you can normally buy them in Asian grocery stores and markets. In Manchester, we have a so-called Curry Mile where you can pick them up. If you cannot get hold of them, you can use dried ones but soak them first in boiling water to soften them.

Kari Ayam dan Daging
Meat Curry Powder

The brand I use is *Adabi*, which is produced and widely available in Malaysia. However, in the UK this curry powder is only available in specialist oriental grocery stores. It comprises a mixture of ground herbs like cumin, coriander, fennel and chilli powder, among others. It is good quality, saving a lot of time with the pestle and mortar.

Kari Ikan
Fish Curry Powder

Similar to the meat version, this is another type of *Adabi* brand but designed for fish curries. I also use this in *Murtabak* (see p75). It is less spicy compared to the meat curry powder.

Kerisik
Roasted Coconut

The authentic way of making this is by frying desiccated coconut until brown and then blending it until the coconut turns into a paste. However, thanks to my best friend Yosrie, he taught me to do it a quicker way by putting the coconut block (creamed coconut) in a microwave oven for 3 minutes. Stir it immediately and microwave for a further minute to make it darker. Like magic, it turns to roasted coconut of the same quality as if it was done authentically. One block of creamed coconut block can produce up to 8 tablespoons of *kerisik*. I get so proud telling my students how they will save time preparing it this way.

Asam Jawa
Tamarind

Malaysians use a lot of tamarind juice in cooking, as an alternative to lime or lemon juice. It gives the same effect. Tamarind is like a sour plum, of which the pulp is edible (when ripened). Soak the tamarind pulp in boiled water for 5 minutes before using it. If the recipe only requires a few tablespoons of the juice, just soak a couple of pinches of tamarind pulp. The remaining can be kept for months in the fridge.

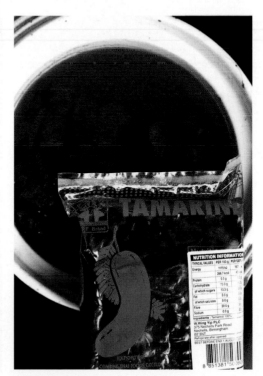

Daun Pandan
Fragrant Screwpine

Pandan leaves are from the 'Screwpine Tree', and are widely used in South East Asian cooking. Their distinctive, slightly nutty aroma adds a delicate scent to rice and added flavour to curries. In Malaysia, their extracted juice is a natural green colouring used for desserts. Tied in a knot, a leaf can also be used to brush oil on a pan.

Sos Cili Manis
Sweet Chilli Sauce

The best sweet chilli sauce brand I have come across is the Thai *Mae Ploy* label. The sauce has less vinegar in it and more garlic. It is nice to have with spring rolls, samosas and also *murtabak* (page 75 for recipe). In Manchester I get this from oriental stores or the world foods aisle of major supermarkets.

Santan
Coconut Milk

There are many brands available in the UK, but the best brand in my opinion is *Chaokoh*, produced in Thailand. It's very creamy and not watery compared to other brands you might pick up in a British supermarket. In Malaysia you can buy fresh coconut milk, which is even better.

Kicap Manis
Sweet Soy Sauce

The brand I normally go for is Malaysian *Habhal's Kicap Kipas Udang*. There are two types available: sweet, with a red label; and salty, with a green label. Many of my recipes use the sweet type.

Belacan
Shrimp Paste

*B*elacan is popular throughout South East Asia, made from fermented ground shrimps which are then sun-dried and formed into slabs like cheese or pâte. These days you can widely buy it in jars. Malaysians use the paste to enhance the flavour, though the smell can really put some Western people off.

Gula Melaka
Dark Coconut Block Sugar

This type of sugar comes in blocks or discs, but is different from palm sugar which is widely available in oriental shops in the UK. The sweetness is more intense compared to granulated white sugar. Malaysians use a lot of coconut block sugar for their desserts. I also choose to use it in my beef *rendang* (page 112 for recipe) as it gives extra darkness to the gravy.

Bawang Goreng
Crispy Fried Shallots

You can buy these ready-made in plastic jars or packets. They are widely used in Malaysia to garnish curries – just sprinkle them over. Curiously enough, Scandinavians enjoy them too. You can even buy them in the food shop of a certain well-known Swedish furniture store.

Rempah Tumis
Whole Mixed Herbs

Whole mixed herbs and seeds are available in many South Asian grocery stores here in Manchester. They come in a packet containing a mixture of black mustard seeds, fennel, fenugreek and cumin seeds. I use them in my *Kari Ikan* (fish curry) recipe on page 84. In Malaysia I love getting these from the specialist spice stall at the local market.

Starters

T he starters in my restaurant are very popular. They are based on Malaysian street food, of which Penang is the capital of Malaysia. I was brought up on good food from local stalls, and so am proud to introduce it to my guests.

When Andy, my business partner, visited Malaysia my parents would drive us – sometimes miles – to the very best places to eat in Penang. My Mum was very particular about the quality of her food, which is where I get that characteristic from. Andy treated her once to a 'tiffin lunch' at a certain 5-star hotel in Georgetown, but she thought it was not as good as her favourite stall, which cost a tenth of the price!

Most Malaysians do not regularly have starters as such. Rather we have appetizers as street food snacks or as part of a family banquet, sharing all the dishes at the same time.

Kerabu Ayam & Mangga

Serves 2

Mango & Chicken Salad

When I introduced this simple but delicious salad for Ning's summer menu, it went down very well with our guests. I made the recipe more fusion than our traditional Malaysian style salad. Back home in Malaysia we normally have sprigs of tapioca, cashew nuts or raw bamboo shoots to name a few, accompanied by sambal belacan *(chilli with shrimp paste). Nothing can beat that. For this fusion recipe I blend in a bit of sesame oil and sweet chilli sauce for the dressing.*

Ingredients

For chicken marinade

200g chicken breast

¼ teaspoon salt

¼ teaspoon ground white pepper

¼ teaspoon ground black pepper

2 tablespoons cooking oil

For salad

½ medium sized ripe mango

2 handfuls mixed crunchy salad

2 tablespoons cashew nuts

½ tablespoon sesame oil

2 tablespoons sweet chilli sauce

1 sprig spring onion

2 sprigs fresh coriander leaves

Using a frying pan, fry the cashew nuts without oil until brown. This will make the nuts crunchier. Set aside.

Cut the chicken breast into thin slices and marinade for 5 minutes with ground black and white pepper and salt. Using the same pan, add cooking oil and fry until the chicken slices are cooked and turned crispy brown.

Peel the mango and cut into julienne strips. Cut the spring onion into pieces about 2cm long and similarly with the coriander leaves.

Using a salad bowl, add all the ingredients for the salad including chicken. Gently mix the ingredients with wooden salad servers.

Serve it right away to maintain the crunchiness of the salad.

Kuah Kacang
Peanut Sauce

Serves 4 small bowls

This was my secret recipe until now! Peanut sauce is best served with chicken satay or prawn fritters (recipes follow in this section). During Hari Raya (Eid al-Fitr Muslim festival) season, we serve this peanut sauce with nasi himpit (rice cakes), which are traditionally cooked in young coconut leaves. Some of my guests in the restaurant prefer to have it with prawn crackers, which makes a change from sweet chill sauce. It is very moreish.

Ingredients

100ml cooking oil

2 tablespoons blended onion

½ tablespoon blended garlic

½ tablespoon blended ginger

4 tablespoons blended lemongrass

4 tablespoons dried chilli paste, refer to page 55

5 tablespoons tamarind juice

3 tablespoons crushed dark coconut block sugar

1 teaspoon salt

1 lemongrass, bruised bottom half

300g peanuts, plain and skinless

400ml water

50ml coconut milk

2 tablespoons dark sweet soy sauce

Heat up a frying pan and fry the peanuts without oil until they turn slightly charred brown (not burnt). Cool down the peanuts before grinding in a food processor – make sure they are totally cooled down otherwise they will not be crunchy. When grinding, make them slightly coarse; not too fine.

Heat up the cooking oil in a saucepan. Fry the blended lemongrass until its sensational aroma rises. Add in the onion, garlic and ginger, and cook until the ingredients start to turn slightly brown. Next add in the dried chilli paste, tamarind juice, coconut block sugar, salt and bruised lemongrass. Bring to the boil on a medium heat and cook the ingredients until the oil separates.

Then add in the peanuts, water, coconut milk and soy sauce. Reduce to a low heat and simmer until the oil separates again. This will take up to 30 minutes. Keep stirring from time to time to avoid the sauce sticking to the pan. The sauce will thicken and the colour will get slightly darker. Take off the heat and you are ready to serve. You can also have the sauce cold, if you prefer.

Sate Ayam
Chicken Satay

Makes approximately 30 skewers

Satay is my all-time favourite. In Kajang (about 30 minutes drive from Kuala Lumpur city centre) there is a place called Sate Kajang Haji Samuri. This is a 'must visit' satay house every time I go back to Malaysia. For my recipe, I use chicken leg meat instead of chicken breast. It tastes better and more succulent; not dry like chicken breast can be. You can use chicken breast if you prefer. Satay is typically served with a legendary spicy peanut sauce, rice cakes, cucumber chunks and red onion slices. See p69 for my peanut sauce recipe.

Ingredients

For satay

1kg chicken leg meat

6 tablespoons blended lemongrass

3 tablespoons turmeric powder

½ tablespoon cumin powder

2 teaspoons salt

3 tablespoons white sugar

30 bamboo satay skewers

1 lemongrass, bruised

1 small bowl cooking oil

For rice cakes

1 cup long grain rice

2 cups water

1 tablespoon cooking oil

½ teaspoon salt

Cling film

For garnishing

Cucumber slices

Tomato slices

Red onions

To prepare the rice cakes, wash and rinse the rice with cold water three times. Boil the rice with 2 cups of water and add salt. Cook for 10 minutes until the rice becomes soft and all the water absorbed. Using a flat deep tray, put cling film (this will avoid the rice cake from sticking to the tray) over the base and sides and pour in the cooking oil and cooked rice. Use a wooden spoon to press the rice very firmly to make it flat and stick together. Set aside to cool down. Cut into cubes when cooled.

For the satay skewers, cut the chicken meat into strips about 10cm long. Add the blended lemongrass, turmeric and cumin powder, salt, sugar and chicken into a bowl. Marinade for at least 2 hours in the fridge. The taste will be much better if marinated overnight. Thread the chicken pieces gently onto the skewers. Repeat until all the meat is skewered. The satay is best cooked using a charcoal grill or barbecue, but you can also use a domestic oven grill. Place the skewered chicken under a hot grill or on the barbecue and, using the bruised lemongrass stalk, brush them with cooking oil to add moisture to the meat. Keep turning the satay sticks to make sure they are evenly cooked. Cook until the meat is cooked through and turns brown with a slight charcoal effect. Serve the skewers with peanut sauce together with the rice cakes, cucumber, onion and tomato slices on the side.

Sotong Berlada

Fresh Peppercorn Stalks Calamari

This dish is one of the most popular starters in my restaurant. It's very simple to do. The thing about cooking calamari (squid) is getting the timing right. How long it is cooked is very important. If overcooked, the texture will turn rubbery and chewy, instead of light and tender.

Ingredients

2 calamari tubes
4 tablespoons plain flour
4 tablespoons self raising flour
1 tablespoon ground white pepper
2 teaspoons white sugar
½ teaspoon salt
750ml cooking oil
Fresh peppercorn stalks (optional)

To get a pattern on the calamari, place it on a chopping board and cut it open to make one flat piece. Place the inside up and cut a diagonal criss-cross pattern halfway through the flesh. Then cut the flat piece into 6 sections.

Separately, add the white pepper, sugar, salt, plain and self raising flour into a mixing bowl. Mix it well. Add the calamari pieces into the bowl and coat them with the flour mixture.

Heat up the cooking oil in a wok or deep frying pan. Make sure the oil is smoky hot before frying the calamari; otherwise the batter will not stick to the calamari. To know whether the oil is ready, fry the fresh peppercorn stalks and if it sizzles, then the oil is ready. Fry the calamari pieces for 30 seconds or until they curl up and change to golden brown.

Serve them with garnish and a sweet chilli sauce dip.

Murtabak
Mamak *Omelette Pancake*

Makes 4 parcels

This is one of the dishes I teach at Ning's Cookery School. The recipe involves a lot of preparation as there are so many ingredients used to cook it. The key ingredient though is the curry powder which gives an added twist compared to a normal omelette. My murtabak *version is slightly different from a typical Malaysian one found at popular* Mamak *stalls. I use spring roll pastry instead of soft pastry like* roti canai *to wrap the omelette. It's much more crunchy.*

Ingredients

For the omelette

4 eggs

2 tablespoons fish curry powder (*Adabi* brand recommended)

4 teaspoons white sugar

2 teaspoons salt

8 tablespoons boiled diced potato

8 tablespoons diced onions

4 chilli slices (optional)

4 tablespoons ready-made fried shallots

8 tablespoons boiled shredded chicken

4 tablespoons spring onions, cut into 1cm wide

For wrapping

1 packet spring roll pastry (size 250 x 250mm)

1 cup water

For frying

Cooking oil

Break the eggs and add all the ingredients in the bowl. Mix it well. Heat up a frying pan and add a little cooking oil. The mixture is for four portions, so there will be four omelette portions to be fried. Using a ladle, pour one portion and fry like a normal omelette. Flip it to cook both sides (don't worry if breaks up a bit) and then set aside. Similarly fry all remaining portions.

To wrap the omelette, peel off two layers of spring roll pastry and place it on a chopping board. Place one omelette portion in the middle and shape it into an even square, leaving a margin of pastry around the edges for you to fold inwards. Cover the corner areas of the square, particularly, as this will stop cooking oil getting inside the parcel and making it oily. Start wrapping the omelette from the bottom edge. Fold up and push in slightly from the crease to make it tighter. Next, fold from the left and right hand edges before folding the top. Dab a bit of water to seal the final fold (top) into a parcel. Repeat for remaining omelette portions.

To cook, heat up the frying pan – this time with less oil. Fry each parcel on both sides starting with the folded side down until they turn crispy brown.

To serve, cut each parcel into four triangles and serve with sweet chilli sauce or curry sauce.

Cucur Udang
Prawn Fritters

Serves 4

My favourite cucur udang stall is in Penang, just off Penang Road and next to Chowratsa Market. The stall has been run by three generations of the same family. I remember going there with my family every time we went to Penang Island for a shopping trip. My recipe of cucur udang is slightly different from the one served at the stall. I use king prawns, and a lot of garlic chives and bean sprouts to give the fritters extra crunchiness. When buying prawns, get the ones with tails on, as this will keep the prawns from being reduced in size when fried.

Ingredients

250g plain flour
50g self raising flour
600ml water
1 teaspoon turmeric
1 teaspoon salt
8 to 12 king prawns
250g bean sprouts
25g garlic/Chinese chives

10 pieces pre-fried tofu
750ml cooking oil to deep fry

For garnishing
Cucumber slices

See page 69 for peanut sauce recipe

Using a big bowl, add the plain and self raising flours, water, turmeric powder and salt. Mix it well.

Heat up the cooking oil in a wok, or deep frying pan if you don't have a wok. Lightly fry the pre-fried tofu for two minutes and set aside.

Add a handful of bean sprouts and coarsely-chopped chives with two or three of the king prawns into the batter. Mix it well and, using your fingers, carefully drop a handful of the battered ingredients into the hot oil. If you're not confident about using your hand – Malaysian style – you can use a ladle to drop the mixture. (Only mix the bean sprouts and chives when you are ready to fry it. If they are left in the batter for a while, they will get soggy.) Fry until the bean sprouts and chives turn brown and the batter looks crispy.

Repeat the same until all the batter is used up.

Serve the fritters with chunky cucumber slices, the fried tofu and homemade peanut sauce dip.

Abdul Azeez, the *cucur udang* stall owner in Georgetown, Penang.

Fish & Seafood

The best thing about fish and seafood in Malaysia is the freshness. You can tell the fish is fresh by looking for a hint of light green on the flesh. Another way of telling is by looking at the eyes – as I said earlier. If the eyes have gone red, then the fish are not fresh.

There is a famous fishing village in *Kuala Muda*, near Butterworth (Penang) where bidding at a fish auction is done in a very unique way. It is done by whispering the bid price to the fishermen, who bring the fish to a busy auction shed straight from their trawlers. The bidders whisper their bids to a fisherman in turns. The fisherman will whisper back the highest bid to the bidders and wait to hear whether each bidder will increase it. So the highest bidder will get the seafood bargained for.

After buying fresh fish, if you want to get rid of the strong fish smell when you get home, use tamarind pulp and salt. Rub it together over the fish and leave aside for a few minutes. Wash it again before cooking.

Ikan Belah Belakang

Serves 2

Pan Fried Mackerel Stuffed with Chilli

My mouth starts watering when I write this recipe. My favourite fish for this recipe is cencaru (torpedo scad) or, as Malaysians translate it, jacket fish because of its thick skin. The flesh of cencaru is quite flaky and the skin is firm so it becomes deliciously crispy when fried. As it is not available fresh in the UK, I use mackerel as an alternative.

Ingredients

2 medium size mackerels, about 400g each

400ml cooking oil to deep fry

For chilli paste filling

6 fresh red chillies, deseeded

½ teaspoon shrimp paste (see page 60)

½ medium size onion

2 tablespoons tamarind juice

2 tablespoons white sugar

Wash and clean the mackerels with salt and tamarind. Slit the backs of the fish along their spine to create a pocket for the chilli paste and set aside.

Using a pestle and mortar, pound all the ingredients for the chilli paste. Start with the chilli, followed by the shrimp paste, onion and sugar. Finally add the tamarind juice and just stir with a spoon to mix it well. This can also be done using a blender or grinder but try to make the paste a little coarse; not too fine.

Now for the fun bit – stuff the chilli paste into the back of each fish.

Heat up the cooking oil in a wok or frying pan. Best to use a non-stick pan or wok so the fish do not stick or break up. When the oil is ready, gently put the fish into the wok and fry until gorgeously crispy brown. Flip to the other side and cook until brown again.

Ready to serve with a crunchy fresh salad or just rice – make sure you enjoy all that lovely chilli paste!

Kari Ikan

Fish Curry

This is a real classic. Traditionally this dish involves a lot of pounding spices, but these days most Malaysian households prefer to use ready-made curry powder. The brand I normally use is a good quality Malaysian curry powder called Adabi which is available in two types: meat or fish curry powders. My hometown Penang is well known for its fish head curry. Every Mamak stall in Penang has fish head curry as their signature dish. For my recipe I use salmon. I experimented with other fish available in the UK, but salmon always came out the best as it blends well with the curry flavours.

Ingredients

8 tablespoons cooking oil

2 tablespoons blended onion

1 tablespoon blended garlic

1 tablespoon blended ginger

2 stalks fresh curry leaves

½ teaspoon whole mixed herbs (see page 61)

3 tablespoons Malaysian *Adabi* fish curry powder powder

4 tablespoons tamarind juice

1 teaspoon salt

1 tablespoon white sugar

125ml water

600g salmon fillets, cut into chunks

50ml coconut milk

6 okra

1 tomato, cut into quarters

Heat up the cooking oil in a saucepan. Add the onion, garlic and ginger. Cook until the aromas rise. Then add in the mixed herbs and fresh curry leaves. Keep the heat low at this stage as the herbs can easily burn if the oil is too hot. Cook until the blended ingredients start turning brown.

Next add the curry powder, tamarind juice, salt, sugar and water. Cook until the oil separates, and continue cooking for a couple of minutes or so before adding the salmon fillets.

When the fillets are about half cooked through, add in the coconut milk, okra and tomato. Simmer on a low heat until the salmon fillets are nicely cooked through but moist.

Ready to serve, with rice of course.

Siput Masak Serai
Mussels in Lemongrass Sauce

Serves 2

My Mum passed this recipe to me but I make it slightly differently. She used siput la la (clams), lemongrass, cut chillies, and Monosodium Glutamate (MSG) – which I despise! I have never liked to use MSG in my food, especially at Ning. Anyway, I remember we went for a family holiday once in Pulan Aman (Aman Island), not far from the Penang Bridge. It was not like a five star hotel; just a simple chalet run by a family there. So as you might expect everything was non-commercialised and still untouched. The thing that excited us about going there was the siput la la. We woke up early in the morning when the tide was low and I was excited and surprised to see clams everywhere, on the mud flats. Normally you have to dig the mud to find them, but what I saw that day was unbelievable. We collected and took home two huge baskets of clams and gave some to the neighbours as there were so many. For this recipe, I use mussels instead of clams. I am a huge fan of mussels as their flesh is bigger and plumper than clams.

Ingredients

1 litre water

3 stalks lemongrass, bruised bottom half

4 cloves garlic, peeled and sliced thinly

1 tablespoon fish sauce

1 bird's eye chilli, chopped

1 teaspoon salt

½ tablespoon white sugar

500g fresh mussels

50ml coconut milk

Fresh coriander leaves and cut chillies to garnish

Clean and get rid of the beard on the mussel shells thoroughly. Check carefully for any mussels that are slightly opened – best to discard them as they might contain mud.

Using a deep cooking pot, pour in the water and bring to the boil. Then add the lemongrass, garlic, fish sauce, bird's eye chilli, salt and sugar and let it all boil for about 5 minutes. You can add more bird's eye chillies if you like your food very spicy.

Next add in the mussels and cook until they start opening up; then quickly pour in the coconut milk and heat up. The coconut milk goes in at the end so that it does not create a layer of oil if overcooked.

Serve in a deep bowl and garnish with cut chillies and fresh coriander leaves.

Ikan Goreng Masam Manis
Sea Bass in Sweet Chilli Tomato Sauce

Serves 2

This is another favourite dish of mine that my Mum gave me. The dish is best cooked with Black Pomfret but I couldn't find it in the market in Manchester. Only Silver Pomfret is available fresh. The silver is less meaty and smaller in size compared to Black Pomfret. So, as an alternative, I use Sea Bass fillets, battered in corn flour seasoned with white pepper, salt and sugar to make it crispy. In Malaysia, this dish (using Black Pomfret) is usually cooked for the bride and groom at wedding receptions. When I introduced this dish on Ning's summer menu, it received rave reviews from food critics – and our customers.

Ingredients

for the sauce

6 tablespoons cooking oil
1 tablespoon blended onion
1 tablespoon blended ginger
1 tablespoon blended garlic
6 fresh chillies, deseeded and ground
   with 120ml water until smooth
240ml tomato ketchup, any brand
250ml water
1 teaspoon salt
100g white sugar
2 medium sized tomatoes, roundly sliced
2 spring onions, cut about 4cm long

2 stalks fresh coriander, cut about
   4cm long

for the sea bass and batter

2 Sea Bass, 300-400g each, filleted
8 tablespoons cornflour
½ teaspoon salt
½ teaspoon white sugar
½ teaspoon ground white pepper
750ml cooking oil to deep fry

Fresh coriander and ready-made
   fried shallots for garnishing

To cook the sauce, heat up the cooking oil in a saucepan. Add in the blended onion, garlic and ginger. Cook until the aromas rise and the ingredients start turning slightly brown. Next add the blended fresh chillies, tomato ketchup, salt, sugar and water. Bring to the boil and keep it boiling for another 5 minutes until the sauce thickens slightly. Set aside.

Mix the cornflour with white pepper, sugar and salt. Sprinkle over a tray or clean flat surface and coat the Sea Bass fillets in the mixture. Heat up the cooking oil in a deep frying pan or wok. Make sure the oil is properly hot before frying the fillets otherwise the batter will not be lightly crispy. Fry them until the batter turns golden brown. Better to fry two fillets at a time to give enough room in the wok or frying pan for the batter to coat the fish well.

Place the fried Sea Bass fillets on the plate, set aside and turn up the heat again for the sauce. Add in the sliced tomatoes, fresh coriander and spring onions, and bring to the boil. Turn off the heat and pour the sauce over the fried Sea Bass. Garnish with fresh coriander and fried shallots to serve.

DAGING RM

TEMENUNG BOREK RM

TELUR IKAN

KELI RM 3.00

PARI RM 7.00

AYAM SEBELAH RM-

TERUBUK SEKERAT Import
Rm
1800-1000

SIAKA

SOTONG
DAGING & AYAM
POTONG DI SINI

Seafood price list at the Seafood Grill Stall in *Kepala Batas*, Butterworth.

Ikan Stim Halia

Steamed Sea Bass

This is another popular favourite at Ning. The fresh ginger flavour brings out the sweetness of the Sea Bass. I have tested this recipe using both Sole and Cod fish but neither of these came out as good as the Sea Bass. At the restaurant we serve it on a bed of steamed spinach, so it's also a very healthy dish for any occasion.

Ingredients

2 Sea Bass, 300-400g each, filleted
¼ teaspoon salt
¼ teaspoon white sugar
¼ teaspoon ground white pepper
500g spinach, cut into 10cm strips

For the sauce
200ml chicken stock (*from one chicken breast with 250ml water seasoned with a pinch of salt and white sugar*)

150ml light soy sauce
4 tablespoons peanut oil
4 tablespoons oyster sauce
½ tablespoon sesame oil
1½ tablespoons white sugar
¼ teaspoon salt
¼ teaspoon ground white pepper
100g fresh ginger root, peeled and cut into julienne strips
4 tablespoons blended garlic

Season the Sea Bass fillets with salt, sugar and ground white pepper. Set aside for 5 minutes.

Using a steamer, place the fillets in the steamer for about 10 minutes, once it has started steaming. Then add in the cut spinach – placing it around the perimeter of the steamer – and steam for a further 5 minutes until the spinach has wilted.

You can cook the sauce while steaming the fillets by adding all the sauce ingredients into a separate saucepan. Bring to the boil and turn to a low heat, simmering for 5 minutes to let the ingredients blend in well. Then turn off the heat and set aside.

Serve the dish in a large soup plate by putting the spinach in first as a bed, followed by the fillets on top. Gently pour over the sauce, and you are ready to serve.

Sambal Udang

Prawns in Chilli Gravy

For Malaysians udang *(prawns) are usually cooked with their heads and shells on. The beauty of it is that you get the excitement of peeling the shell off to reveal the juicy meaty prawn inside, which is the reward. Most tiger and king prawns available in the UK are frozen, but buy fresh ones if you can. The thick sauce – gravy – for this dish is not as spicy as you might think by looking at the photograph. The added tamarind juice 'kills' the strong sharp chilli spiciness and blends so well that you can taste a hint of the sourness of the tamarind. I prefer to use paste from dried chillies in most of my recipes because it is sweeter, more intense and less sharp than fresh chillies and the crimson colour is so rich, making the dish beautifully presented.*

Ingredients

16 tiger or king prawns, peeled and
   deveined

100ml cooking oil

4 tablespoons blended onion

1 tablespoon blended garlic

1 tablespoon blended ginger

125ml dried chilli paste (see page 55)

100ml tamarind juice

150ml water

1 teaspoon shrimp paste

4 tablespoons white sugar

1 teaspoon salt

1 carrot, peeled and cut into julienne
   strips

8 kaffir lime leaves

Heat up a wok or saucepan and add in the cooking oil. Add the blended onion, garlic and ginger. Cook until the aromas rise.

Next add the kaffir lime leaves and cook for another 2 minutes. Stir in the chilli paste, tamarind juice, sugar, salt, shrimp paste and only half the water portion. Stir the ingredients well, especially the shrimp paste; make sure it is totally blended. Simmer on a low heat until the oil separates. This will give time for the chilli to be cooked properly. The gravy will thicken at this stage.

Turn the heat back up to full and add in the prawns, carrot and the remaining water. Cook until the prawns turn pink. This dish is best served with jasmine rice.

Udang Masak Kunyit
Stir-fried Turmeric Prawns

Serves 2

This is a really simple stir-fried dish that is perfect for a quick mid-week meal. It works well cooking it on a high fiery heat like you see in many oriental restaurants. The turmeric is an essential Malay ingredient and as I like my food really colourful I add in carrots and fine beans, though you could easily experiment with other vegetables.

Ingredients

14 tiger or king prawns, peeled and deveined

100ml cooking oil

2 tablespoons blended onion

1 tablespoon blended garlic

1 tablespoon blended ginger

1 teaspoon turmeric powder

1 tablespoon ground black pepper

1 chilli, deseeded and cut into strips

1 tablespoon white sugar

1 teaspoon salt

50ml tamarind juice

125ml water

1 carrot, peeled and cut into julienne strips

100g fine beans, cut into 4cm long

½ medium sized onion, thinly sliced

Heat up a wok or frying pan and add in the cooking oil. Add the blended onion, garlic and ginger, and cook until the aromas rise. Next add in the turmeric powder and black pepper, chilli, sugar, salt, tamarind juice and only half the water portion.

Cook until the sauce is slightly reduced and begins to thicken. Add in the carrot, fine beans and sliced onions, and cook for another two minutes to soften them. Finally drop in the prawns and cook them until they turn pink. Turn off the heat and you are ready to serve.

I think this dish is best served with egg fried rice.

AYAM KAMPUNG 1KG RM.

AYAM DAGING 1KG RM

Fresh chicken stall.

Meat &
Poultry

Most Malaysians are big meat eaters – especially of chicken which is cheaper and widely available. We do not have Malaysian lamb but sometimes have goat, which I am not so keen on.

When I was about 7 years old, I remember all the chickens in our backyard at home in the village. My parents used to get me, as I was small, to go and get the eggs and sometimes the angry chickens would peck me in the process for stealing their eggs.

We use most parts of a chicken. Most Malaysians are brought up not to waste food. Many curries are served with chicken on the bone, not deboned chicken like from supermarkets. We use the chicken stock for soups and cooking rice in.

Daging Masak Kicap
Beef in Soy Sauce

Serves 2

This dish has more of an Indian Muslim (Mamak) influence. Every Mamak stall you go to in Malaysia serves this dish. Some put honey in it, but I choose not to as I use sweet soy sauce; so the sweetness is adequate. The curry leaves, fried onion and ginger garnish help bring out the aroma. You can use chicken instead of beef if you prefer, but with chicken it is better marinated with turmeric, salt and sugar and then deep fried first.

Ingredients

For the beef and gravy

500g beef, topside, cut into thin slices

6 tablespoons cooking oil

2 tablespoons blended onion

1 tablespoon blended garlic

1 tablespoon blended ginger

1 cinnamon bark, about 5cm long

2 star anise

4 cardamon seeds

1 *pandan* leaf (tied in a knot)

1 tablespoon meat curry powder
   (Malaysian *Adabi* curry powder)

1 tablespoon white sugar

½ teaspoon salt

50ml water

6 tablespoons sweet soy sauce
   (I recommend *Habhal's Kicap Kipas Udang* Malaysian product)

150ml water (use with the beef)

1 tablespoon coconut milk

4 baby or new potatoes

Cooking oil to deep fry potatoes

For garnishing

4 tablespoons cooking oil

1 stalk fresh curry leaves

1 tablespoon ginger slices, julienne style

1 medium size red onion, cut into rings

Peel and cut the potatoes about 1cm thick. Soak the sliced potatoes in water for about 5 minutes, to remove some starch. Drain the water and dab with kitchen paper towel before frying. Deep fry the potatoes in cooking oil until they begin to turn brown. Set aside.

Heat up 6 tablespoons cooking oil in a saucepan. Add the blended onion, garlic and ginger. Fry until the aromas rise. Next add in the cinnamon bark, star anise, cardamon seeds and *pandan* leaf. Keep frying until the mixture turns golden brown. Add the curry powder, salt, sugar and 50ml of water. Cook until the oil starts to separate from the other ingredients. Keep cooking for another couple of minutes. Now add in the beef, soy sauce, 150ml of water and the coconut milk. Simmer for 20 minutes on a medium heat until the beef is tender and the gravy has thickened. Turn off the heat and add in the fried potatoes, stirring well. Set aside.

For the garnish, heat up the oil in a small saucepan, adding in the onion, ginger and curry leaves. Fry until the onion rings turn brown. Scoop the ingredients out and sprinkle over the beef dish, ready to serve.

Rendang Pedas Ayam
My Mum's Chicken Rendang

Serves 6

In Malaysia there are many different types of rendang, possibly the most well-known Malaysian dish other than satay. Different regions of Malaysia have their own style of rendang. Even our neighbouring country, Indonesia, has their own version. This recipe is purely my Mum's recipe. Not adjusted like my version of beef rendang, I call her way the lazy way of doing rendang as you put in all the ingredients in one go. Unfortunately this recipe does not work well using chicken breasts as the dish needs to be simmered for quite a long time, making the chicken go dry and tough. So my recommendation is to use a whole chicken on the bone. Not many people are so keen about that but, trust me, the taste is a lot better than using chicken breasts. The only ingredient that I have to replace from my Mum's original recipe is the turmeric leaf – use kaffir lime leaves instead. I have searched everywhere in Manchester and can't find it. In the end I may have to grow one myself using a turmeric bulb from the Thai grocery store!

Ingredients

1 whole chicken, about 1.5kg and cut into 12 pieces
2 tablespoons white sugar
1 teaspoon salt
2 tablespoons tamarind juice
2 stalks lemongrass, bruised
200ml water
400ml coconut milk, canned
6 fresh kaffir lime leaves
2 tablespoons *kerisik* (roasted coconut, see page 57)

To blend

20 dried chillies, soaked in boiled water for 10 minutes to soften
1 galangal root, about 5cm long, peeled
2 stalks lemongrass
4 cloves garlic
8 shallots
1 small ginger root, about 2cm long, peeled
½ medium sized onion
100ml water

Clean the chicken pieces and put aside.

Blend the chillies, galangal, two stalks lemongrass, garlic, shallots, onion and ginger. Add 100ml of water to ease the blending process.

Heat up a wok or suitable saucepan. No oil required. Add in the blended ingredients, chicken, coconut milk, 200ml of water, sugar, salt, tamarind juice and bruised lemongrass. Bring to the boil and then turn down the heat to medium.

Simmer for about an hour, stirring from time to time to avoid the gravy from sticking to the pan. Cook until the gravy has thickened and the oil separated. Finally add in the kaffir lime leaves and *kerisik*. Stir well and cook for another 5 minutes. Turn off the heat and you're ready to serve, with a sprinkling of Malaysian crispy fried shallots on top.

Gulai Ayam
Malay Chicken Curry

Serves 2

Malaysians cook curries on a daily basis and the type they eat varies. A daily meal will not be complete without having curry and rice. Most will have it for lunch too. My gulai version is slightly different from many Malaysian households'. I make my sauce thicker than the usual style because, for me, there is more flavour to it. You can use prawns, beef or just vegetables for this recipe. For vegetarian curry, I recommend sweet potato, aubergines and butternut squash.

Ingredients

400g chicken breast, thinly sliced

3 tablespoons Malaysian meat curry powder (Malaysian *Adabi* brand preferred)

8 tablespoons cooking oil

2 tablespoons blended onion

1 ½ tablespoons blended garlic

1 ½ tablespoons blended ginger

2 star anise

1 cinnamon bark, about 5cm long

1 *pandan* leaf (tied in a knot)

1 tablespoon white sugar

1 teaspoon salt

100ml water

3 tablespoons tamarind juice

100ml coconut milk

4 baby potatoes, cut into 4 pieces each

1 carrot

Wash the chicken breast and cut into thin slices. I prefer to cut the chicken into thin slices so the meat can absorb the flavour and taste better. Set aside.

Peel the potatoes and carrots. Cut the potatoes into four pieces each and slice the carrots about 1cm thick.

Heat up the oil in a saucepan and add the blended onion, garlic and ginger. Cook until the aromas rise. Next add in the star anise, cinnamon bark and *pandan* leaf. Cook until the ingredients start turning brown, then add in the curry powder, water, salt, sugar and tamarind juice. Cook until the oil separates from the rest of the ingredients.

Add in the chicken pieces, potato and carrot. Simmer on a medium heat until the chicken is nicely cooked through. This will take about 15 minutes. Add in the coconut milk and bring to boil. Turn off the heat and you are ready to serve.

Kurma Daging

Serves 2

Beef Korma

This dish is different from the Indian Korma that is widely available in the UK. The flavour is heavily infused with ground coriander, cumin and cardamon seeds. I choose to cook this dish with beef. You can use chicken or goat instead of beef, if you prefer. This is one of the dishes served at a Malay wedding.

Ingredients

400g beef, topside and cut about 1cm thick against the grain

6 tablespoons cooking oil

2 tablespoons blended onion

1 tablespoon blended garlic

1 tablespoon blended ginger

4 cardamon seeds

4 cloves

1 star anise

1 cinnamon bark, about 5cm long

1 *pandan* leaf

4 tablespoons Malaysian *kurma* curry powder (*Adabi* brand recommended)

2 tablespoons tamarind juice

1 tablespoon white sugar

¾ teaspoon salt

Mixture 1: 50ml coconut milk and 100ml water

Mixture 2: 50ml coconut milk and 150ml water

1 medium sized red onion, cut into 8 pieces

4 baby or new potatoes, peeled and cut into 4 pieces each

1 small carrot, peeled and each cut into 5cm wedges

1 tomato, cut into quarters

2 stalks mint leaves

Heat up the oil in a saucepan. Add the blended onion, garlic, ginger, cardamon seeds, cloves, star anise, cinnamon bark and *pandan* leaf. Cook until the aromas rise.

Add in the *kurma* curry powder, tamarind juice, salt, sugar and mixture 1 (50ml coconut milk and 100ml water). Cook until the oil separates above the other ingredients.

Next add in the beef pieces and mixture 2 (50ml coconut milk and 150ml water), stirring well. Simmer on a low heat for about 30 minutes. This will make the beef tender and absorb the flavours of the spices. Half way during simmering, put in the potato and carrot.

Once the beef is tender, add in the tomato and cut onion. Bring to the boil and cook for a further 5 minutes. Turn off the heat and stir in some fresh mint leaves.

Ready to serve, with a sprig of mint and cut chilli as garnish.

Ayam Masak Merah

Serves 2

Chicken in Aromatic Chilli & Tomato Sauce

This dish is an all-time favourite for wedding receptions – and one of the most popular dishes in my restaurant. The sauce is infused with star anise, cinnamon and pandan leaves, making it so aromatic. I remember the day my sister got married and my Mum cooked masak merah as one of the dishes. More than 2,000 guests (yes, two thousand) were invited so you can imagine all the preparation involved! It's a Malaysian tradition for the host to invite friends, family and the whole neighbourhood, irrespective of people's ethnic background.

Ingredients

400g chicken breast, thinly sliced

4 tablespoons dried chilli paste

4 tablespoons tomato purée

2 tablespoons blended onions

1 tablespoon blended garlic

1 tablespoon blended ginger

1 *pandan* leaf (tied in a knot)

2 star anise

2 cinnamon bark, about 5cm long

2 tablespoon tamarind juice

1 tablespoon white sugar

1 teaspoon salt

6 tablespoons cooking oil

50ml water

2 tomatoes, cut into quarters

3 tablespoons frozen peas

Heat up the cooking oil in a saucepan. Add the blended onion, garlic and ginger, and cook until the aromas rise. Next add the *pandan* leaf, star anise and cinnamon bark. Keep cooking until the blended ingredients start turning slightly brown.

Add the chilli paste, tomato puree, tamarind juice, sugar and salt. Cook on a medium heat until the oil separates. Stir in the chicken and water, simmering on a low heat until the chicken is cooked through.

Finally add in the cut tomatoes and frozen peas, cooking for a further 5 minutes. Take off the heat and you are ready to serve.

Rendang Daging
Beef Rendang

Serves 2

This dish is the pride of Malaysia. Our Hari Raya *(the Muslim festival of Eid al-Fitr) is celebrated with* rendang *served with* lemang *(glutinous rice and coconut milk grilled in cut bamboo). It is a time-consuming dish as it involves long simmering, but the result is outstanding. It's heavily infused with lemongrass and rich in coconut flavour. There are many versions of* rendang *in Malaysia but I make mine a lot simpler – especially with my 'secret' method of doing* kerisik *(roasted coconut) which gives* rendang *its unique taste sensation!*

Ingredients

6 tablespoons cooking oil

6 tablespoons blended lemongrass

2 tablespoons blended galangal

1 tablespoon blended onion

1 tablespoon blended garlic

1 tablespoon blended ginger

4 tablespoons dried chilli paste
  (refer to page 55)

4 tablespoons tamarind juice

1 tablespoon white sugar

1 teaspoon salt

½ tablespoon dark coconut sugar
  block, broken into small pieces

100ml water (1st part)

500g beef, topside, cut into thin slices

1 lemongrass (use bottom half and bruised)

4 tablespoons coconut milk

100ml water (2nd part)

4 kaffir lime leaves

2 tablespoons *kerisik* (roasted coconut,
  see page 57)

Heat up the cooking oil in a saucepan. Add the blended lemongrass and galangal. Cook for 5 minutes until the aroma rises. Next add the blended onion, garlic and ginger. Cook for a further 5 minutes until it turns brown. Add the blended chilli paste, tamarind juice, white sugar, salt and dark coconut sugar. Cook until the oil separates.

Next add the fresh beef, bruised lemongrass and 1st part water and simmer on a low heat until dry. Once dried, add the coconut milk and 2nd part water and simmer again on a low heat until dry and the oil separates. The simmering in total takes about an hour. This will make the beef tender and give it plenty of time to absorb the rich flavours of the other ingredients.

Finally add the kaffir lime leaves and *kerisik* (roasted coconut) and cook for a further 5 minutes until the *kerisik* has blended in well.

Ready to serve with rice.

Sambal Hati Ayam
Chicken Liver in Chilli Sauce

Serves 2

I get a mixed response from my friends whenever I mention about cooking chicken livers; though Andy, my business partner, raves about them. Even my kitchen staff give me the same look I give someone talking about eating chicken feet. So I would assume that this dish will not be everyone's favourite! I guess the chicken livers' slightly rubbery texture is what puts some people off. For my recipe though I fry the livers marinated in turmeric until crispy, and cook in a chilli gravy to give them an extra kick – totally different; really delicious.

Ingredients

750g chicken livers

For marinade

2 teaspoons turmeric powder

½ teaspoon salt

½ teaspoon white sugar

200ml cooking oil for frying

For gravy

6 tablespoons cooking oil used for frying the chicken livers

2 tablespoons blended onion

½ tablespoon blended garlic

½ tablespoon blended ginger

4 tablespoons chilli paste

4 tablespoons tomato ketchup

2 tablespoons tamarind juice

½ teaspoon shrimp paste

1 tablespoon white sugar

½ teaspoon salt

1 carrot, cut into 5cm long wedges

5 fine beans, cut about 5cm long

1 medium sized onion, cut into rings

Marinate the chicken livers with turmeric powder, salt and sugar, and set aside for 10 minutes.

Heat up the oil in a frying pan and fry the chicken livers until they turn crispy dark brown. When frying them, be extra careful as the oil can pop and spit.

To prepare the gravy, scoop out 6 tablespoons of oil used to fry the livers and put into a saucepan. Add the blended onion, garlic and ginger. Fry until the aromas rise. Next add in the chilli paste, tomato ketchup, shrimp paste, tamarind juice, salt and sugar. Cook until the oil separates. Add in the fine beans, carrot and cut onions and stir well. Cook for five minutes. Finally add in the fried chicken livers and cook for another 5 minutes to get the gravy coating all the livers. Ready to serve.

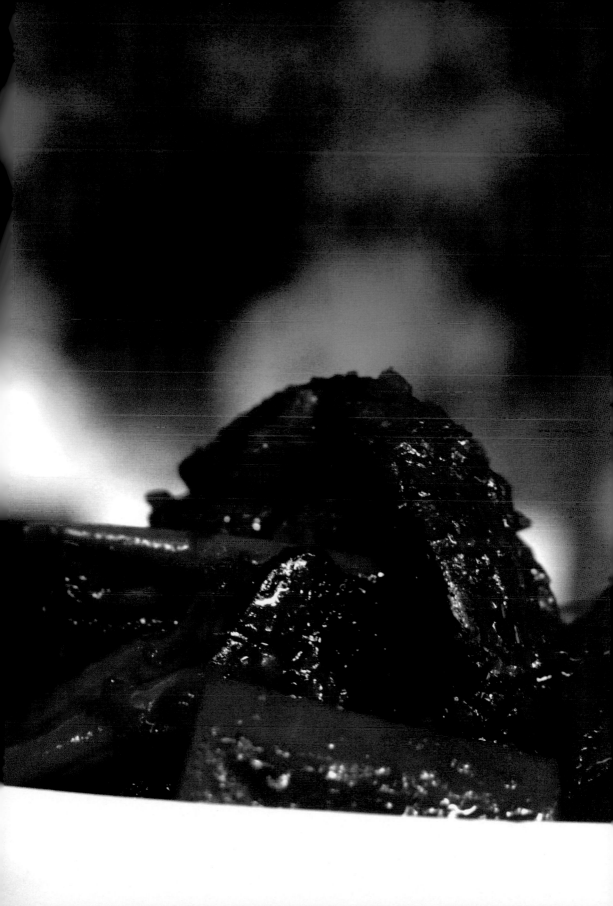

Kari Nyonya
Nyonya Lime Chicken

Serves 2

My knowledge of Malaysian food was so little before I came to the UK to further my studies. I wasn't even aware of Nyonya food when I was in Malaysia. Maybe I was so busy studying to get much time to travel or go out when I was young. Those are the only excuses that I can think of. Their unique and flavoursome dishes are so hard to miss; exactly how I would describe this dish. This is the recipe that I demonstrated on my first TV appearance in the UK.

My friend took me to his favourite Nyonya restaurant called The Bird in Menjalara, Kuala Lumpur. Words cannot describe how exquisite the food was. The restaurant is famously known for its great food, but also its karaoke. One of the owners sings in the restaurant; something I don't think I would have the guts to do in my restaurant – it would definitely drive the customers away!

Ingredients

500g chicken breast
6 tablespoons cooking oil
2 tablespoons blended lemongrass
2 tablespoons blended onion
½ tablespoon blended garlic
½ tablespoon ginger
2 tablespoons dried chilli paste
   (refer to page 55)
½ teaspoon turmeric powder

4 tablespoons tamarind juice
½ teaspoon salt
½ tablespoon white sugar
100ml water
4 kaffir lime leaves
50ml coconut milk
1 lemongrass, bruised
1 tomato, cut into quarters

Heat up the cooking oil in a saucepan. Add the blended onion, garlic, ginger and lemongrass, and cook until the aromas rise.

Next add in the chilli paste, turmeric powder, tamarind juice, salt, sugar, kaffir lime leaves and bruised lemongrass. Cook on a medium heat until the oil separates.

Add in the fresh chicken; simmer on a low heat until the chicken is cooked. Add in the water bit by bit while simmering the chicken. Then add the coconut milk and tomato. Bring to the boil and continue cooking for a further 5 minutes.

Ready to serve.

Georgetown, Penang.

Vegetables

Malaysia is blessed to be so abundant with a wide variety of familiar and less familiar vegetables. We use every part – root, stalk, leaves, seeds and flowers. Turmeric and ginger are good examples. Chillies though are most famous with Asian cooking – we love our food hot! But few people are aware that chillies – chilli peppers – actually originate from the Americas. We largely have the Portuguese to thank for bringing them to South East Asia centuries ago.

Much of our fresh produce is still produced regionally, especially if you go to the local markets. I especially love going to the night markets. We visit them as early as 6pm, and they often line busy roads on the outskirts of towns and villages. They get very noisy with scooters and motorbikes and customers bargaining with the traders. Vegetables line the stalls making them very colourful under the electric lights.

I really hope that Malaysia never loses its colourful and vibrant markets, which are so important to our culture and communities.

Gulai Dalca
Malay Dhal Curry

This delicious, simple vegetable and lentil curry is our nation's favourite to eat with roti canai. *The version served with* roti canai *however is lighter compared to my recipe, which is rich with different types of vegetables. So you can make more of a meal of this if you prefer.*

Ingredients

300g yellow split peas or 'chana dhal', soaked overnight
1 litre water

For the gravy:
1 ½ tablespoon Malaysian curry powder designed for meat dishes
½ teaspoon turmeric powder
150ml coconut milk
75ml tamarind juice
2 cinnamon barks, about 5cm long each
2 star anise
1 *pandan* leaf (tied in a knot)
2 teaspoons salt
¾ tablespoon white sugar

For the vegetables:
1 medium sized potato, chopped into cubes
1 carrot, cut into 4cm long wedges
1 purple aubergine, cut into 8 pieces
1 small unripe mango
2 green chillies, split in half
100g fine beans, cut into 4cm long

For garnishing:
6 tablespoons cooking oil
½ medium sized red onion, cut into rings
3 dried chillies
2 stalks fresh curry leaves

Soak the lentils in cold water overnight to soften them. When ready to cook, drain the water and set aside.

Bring to the boil 1 litre of water and add in the lentils. Boil them until the water is reduced to half. At this stage the lentils will turn soft and become slightly mushy. Add in all the gravy ingredients and bring back to the boil. Cook for a further 5 minutes and then add in all the vegetable ingredients. Cook for a further 15 minutes or until the potato and aubergine go soft. Turn off the heat and set aside. Prepare the garnish before serving.

For the garnish, heat up the oil in a small saucepan, adding in the onion, dried chillies and curry leaves. Fry until the onion rings turn brown. Scoop the ingredients out and sprinkle over the curry, ready to serve.

Sayur Taugeh dan Kucai

Serves 2

Bean Sprouts & Chives in Coconut Milk

Malaysians have this as a side dish. This recipe is fairly simple to do and doesn't take long to prepare – the cooking time is less than five minutes. Chinese chives – or some people call them garlic chives – are different in size and flavour to the chives you see in a British supermarket. They are similar in size to spring onions but the leaves are flat not round. The taste is very garlicky if you eat them raw but once you have cooked them with other ingredients, the taste lessens slightly. They work really well with bean sprouts which are quite tasteless alone. For this recipe I use pre-fried tofu (bean curd), which is available in a packet, dry, from the chiller cabinet.

Ingredients

4 tablespoons cooking oil

4 cloves garlic, thinly sliced

4 shallots, thinly sliced

½ medium sized red onion, cut into
  rings

250g bean sprouts

50g garlic/Chinese chives, cut about
  4cm long

6 pre-fried *tofu*, cut into halves

 ½ large chilli, deseeded and
  cut into strips

50ml coconut milk

100ml water

½ teaspoon salt

1 teaspoon white sugar

Wash the chives and bean sprouts, and set aside.

Heat up the cooking oil in a wok or frying pan. Add in the garlic, shallots and onion rings. Cook until they turn brown. Then add in all the remaining ingredients and cook for a further 5 minutes until the bean sprouts turn slightly soft. Simple!

Ready to serve on the side with your curry.

Pajeri Nenas
Sweet Pineapple Curry

Serves 2

This recipe is similar to gulai *(Malay curry)* but the twist is that kerisik *(roasted coconut)* is added towards the end to give an extra coconut flavour. When choosing the pineapple to cook, choose a ripe one as it will be sweeter. Taste the pineapple before cooking it; if it is a bit sour, then there is no need to add the tamarind juice. The pineapple can also be replaced with aubergine. If you prefer things spicier, add a green chilli split in half to give an extra kick.

Ingredients

½ **ripe sweet pineapple** (about 500g)

100ml cooking oil

2 tablespoons blended onion

1 tablespoon blended garlic

1 tablespoon blended ginger

2 cinnamon barks, about 5cm long

2 star anise

4 cardamon seeds

1 *pandan* leaf (tied in a knot)

3 tablespoons Malaysian curry powder designed for meat dishes

100ml water

2 tablespoons white sugar

1 teaspoon salt

2 tablespoons tamarind juice

100ml coconut milk

2 tablespoons *kerisik* (roasted coconut see page 57)

Peel the pineapple, cut into half lengthways and slice into semi-circular portions about 1cm thick. Set aside.

Heat up the oil in a saucepan and add in the blended onion, garlic and ginger. Cook until the aromas rise. Next add in the star anise, cinnamon barks, cardamon seeds and *pandan* leaf. Continue to cook, stirring as required, until the ingredients start to turn brown. Then add in the curry powder, water, salt, sugar and tamarind juice. Cook until the oil separates from the rest of the ingredients.

Add in the pineapple slices and simmer on a low heat for a further 5 minutes, also adding in the coconut milk. Bring to the boil. Then add in the 'magic ingredient' *kerisik* (roasted coconut) and simmer on a low heat until the oil separates again. This can take up to 15 minutes. Turn off the heat once the oil has separated, and it is ready to serve.

Gado Gado
Indonesian-style Warm Vegetable Salad

Serves 2

This dish has more of an Indonesian influence. I have seen many styles of gado gado wherever I travel, so I have learnt there is no real restriction on what vegetables to include. I make my recipe simple and colourful. If you have eaten gado gado before you will know that traditionally it is served with boiled eggs, but I don't include them. I choose to serve it this way in my restaurant so that Vegans can enjoy it, but feel free to add egg to yours. If you like to try alternative ingredients you can also use cucumber (served raw), green and red peppers or tempe (fermented soya bean cake).

Ingredients

100g spinach, cut about 10cm long

4 baby or new potatoes

4 pre-fried *tofu* pieces, each cut into half

200g bean sprouts

100g fine beans, cut into 4cm long

1 carrot, cut into 4cm long wedge

1 litre water

For garnishing

See page 69 for peanut sauce recipe

Prepare the peanut sauce (see page 69).

Peel the potatoes and cut into quarters. Bring 1 litre of water to the boil and then boil the potato until soft. Next add in all the remaining vegetable ingredients and poach them for about 5 minutes or until the spinach and bean sprouts have gone slightly soft.

Scoop out onto a plate and pour the warm peanut sauce on top, and garnish. Serve it while it is still hot. If you choose to add the boiled egg, just place the egg slices on top of the poached vegetables before pouring the peanut sauce.

Bayam & Cendawan Goreng
Spinach, Tofu & Mushroom Stir Fry

This dish is more of Chinese influence and is normally cooked using oyster sauce. I introduced this in my restaurant as a Vegan dish by using mushroom sauce instead. Most Malaysian Chinese use more garlic in their dishes than Malays, who prefer to use a combination of shallots, onions, ginger and garlic. This dish is best cooked using a fiery heat and takes less than 10 minutes to cook. Very simple.

Ingredients

50ml cooking oil

2 tablespoons garlic, blended

1 carrot, thinly sliced

1 medium sized onion, thinly sliced

50g dried shitake mushroom, soaked in boiled water for 10 minutes

2 teaspoons sesame oil

100ml thick vegetarian mushroom sauce (Oyster sauce alternative)

100ml water

½ tablespoon white sugar

½ teaspoon salt

200g spinach, cut about 10cm long

8 pre-fried *tofu* pieces, each cut in half

Heat up the cooking oil in a wok or frying pan. Add in the blended garlic and cook until its pungent aroma rises. Add in the carrot, onion and soaked shitake mushrooms. Cook for a further 2 minutes. Next add in the sesame oil, mushroom sauce, water, sugar, salt, spinach and *tofu*. Stir-fry until the spinach has wilted and the sauce thickened. This will take between 5 to 8 minutes. Turn off the heat and serve with plain boiled rice or as a side dish.

Rice &
Noodles

It goes without saying that *nasi* (rice) is a staple food of South East Asia. In Malaysia, we eat it at any time of the day, with most of our meals. Kedah, the state immediately to the north of Penang where I am from, is the rice bowl of Malaysia. My grandparents had paddy fields and I remember when I was young visiting them during the harvest season.

We eat it in all kinds of ways – plain, coconut, tomato, byriani, colourful (even blue) – to name just a few.

We also love noodles. They are particularly characteristic of Malaysian Chinese food, whether fried, steamed or in soups. The most popular noodle dish is simply *mee goreng* (fried noodles).

Noodles mostly come in rice or egg varieties, sometimes fresh for dishes like *Keow Teow Goreng* or dry like vermicelli.

Nasi Putih

Plain Boiled Rice

Many of my cookery students in the UK ask me how to cook the rice properly so it is fluffy. I have noticed over here that many people cook the rice by boiling it like pasta and then draining the water, which is very different to what we do in Malaysia. There is a technique to how you measure the exact amount of water required for the rice. The Malaysian way of doing this is easy. Here I show you how. Essentially, we use our index finger to measure the amount of water which should similar to the amount of rice. For Basmati rice, add an additional quarter cup of water. From my experience, Basmati rice tends to be a lot drier than Jasmine or long grain rice.

Ingredients
2 cups long grain or Thai fragrant jasmine rice

2 cups water – measure the depth of the rice in the cooking pot (or rice cooker) by using your index finger and then marking the level on the finger using your thumb; the water level should be the same again above the level of the rice.

1 *pandan* leaf (optional, tied in a knot)

Rinse the rice with cold water in a deep cooking pot (you will need a lid) – preferably non stick – about three times, changing the water each time. You will see the water will get much clearer compared to the first time you wash it. Cook on a medium heat, with lid on, and bring to the boil. Open the lid slightly once it starts boiling and let it simmer until the water has been completely absorbed and the rice turns fluffy. This should take about 10 minutes depending on the quantity. Set aside for five minutes before serving. If you cook with jasmine rice, the rice will be a little lumpy and slightly sticky.

Nasi Lemak
Coconut Rice

Serves 4

Nasi lemak *is our nation's favourite. If you ask most Malaysians what they have for breakfast, it will be either* roti canai *or* nasi lemak. *My Mum used to have a stall selling* nasi lemak *with anchovy* sambal *and long beans in a curry sauce. She would get up at 4am to cook it before selling it from 6am. The smell of* nasi lemak *was what woke me up every morning for school. Malay coconut rice is different to typical Thai coconut rice that you find in many Thai restaurants in the UK.*

Ingredients

2 cups basmati rice, can be replaced with long grain rice

½ cups water

1½ cup coconut milk (I recommend Thai *Chaokoh* brand)

1 tablespoon ginger root, 2 inches long, peeled and cut into julienne strips

2 star anise

1 cinnamon bark, 2 inches long

4 cardamon seeds

1 *pandan* leaf (tied in a knot)

½ teaspoon salt

1 teaspoon white sugar

Wash and rinse the rice in a pot about three times or until the water runs clear, like the boiled rice recipe. Add all the ingredients, including coconut milk, and stir. Cook on a medium heat, bringing it to the boil. Once boiled, turn down the heat, letting it simmer until the rice has gone fluffy. Stir it with a wooden or plastic spoon. Take off the heat and set aside for 10 minutes before serving.

This *nasi lemak* will go well with *sambal udang* (page 94) and *gulai ayam* (page 107).

Nasi Goreng Cina

Serves 2

Chinese Egg Fried Rice

This nasi goreng dish is very simple to cook. I learnt this from a Chinese friend in the UK a few years back and introduced this in my restaurant. The hint of sesame oil and white pepper makes it so aromatic.

Ingredients

2 cups boiled rice

4 tablespoons cooking oil

1 tablespoon garlic, crushed

1 teaspoon sesame oil

1 egg

1 cup spring onions, 1cm long pieces

½ tablespoon light soy sauce

1 teaspoon ground white pepper

1 teaspoon white sugar

½ teaspoon salt

Crispy fried shallots to garnish
   (optional)

Heat up the cooking oil in a wok or non-stick pan. Fry the crushed garlic and sesame oil until the fragrance rises. Break the eggs and fry, stirring them to make them like scrambled eggs. Then add the boiled rice and spring onions, stirring it all thoroughly. Next add the light soy sauce, white pepper, sugar and salt. Fry until all the ingredients have mixed well.

Garnish with crispy fried shallots for serving.

Bihun Goreng Hailam
Fresh Peppercorn Fried Noodles

Serves 2

This stir-fried noodles recipe is of more Malaysian Chinese influence. It was very popular every morning at my Mum's stall. The noodles are best served with soy sauce and chopped bird's eye chillies which will give an extra kick. I use fresh peppercorn stalks for this recipe but you can use dried peppercorns as an alternative.

Ingredients

4 tablespoons cooking oil

2 tablespoons garlic, crushed

1 teaspoon fresh peppercorns, crushed

½ teaspoon ground white pepper

2 eggs

50ml water

10 tiger or king prawns

200g bean sprouts

½ teaspoon salt

2 teaspoons white sugar

2 tablespoons fish sauce

400g thin rice noodles (vermicelli)

½ carrot, cut into julienne strips

2 stalks spring onions, cut 4cm long

½ medium sized onion, sliced

For the bird's eye chilli dip

4 bird's eye chillies

50ml light soy sauce

Soak the rice noodles in boiled water for 5 minutes. Drain the water immediately and run with cold water so the noodles will not turn mushy. Set aside.

To prepare the bird's eye chilli dip, chop the chillies about 1cm wide and pour in the sweet soy sauce. Set aside for serving.

Heat up the cooking oil in a wok or deep frying pan. Add the crushed garlic and cook until the aroma rises. Add the crushed peppercorns and ground white pepper. Next break the eggs and scramble them in with the ingredients. Cook until the scrambled eggs start turn slightly brown. Then add the prepared rice noodles, carrot, spring onions, sliced onion and water. Stir well to mix in all the ingredients.

Cook for 5 minutes on a medium heat. Keep stirring to avoid the ingredients from sticking to the bottom of the wok. Next add in the prawns, bean sprouts, salt, sugar and fish sauce, and cook until the prawns turn pink. Turn off the heat and you are ready to serve with the chilli dip on the side.

Keow Teow Goreng

Serves 2

Stir-fried Thick Rice Noodles

There is a famous large roadside stall in Butterworth, back home, selling Keow Teow Goreng Kerang. *It is one of my family's favourite places to go. They have more than 10 chefs mainly cooking this one dish – fried noodles with cockles. For this recipe, I use juicy mussels instead of cockles.*

Ingredients

4 tablespoons cooking oil

1 tablespoon onion, blended

½ tablespoons garlic, crushed or
   blended

½ tablespoon ginger, blended

2 tablespoons oyster sauce

2 tablespoons chilli paste (can be
   sambal oelek or dried chilli paste)

1 tablespoon dark sweet soy sauce

200g mussels

1 teaspoon salt

¾ tablespoon white sugar

50ml water

400g flat rice noodles, 5mm wide

½ medium sized onion, sliced

1 stalk spring onions

50g green beans, cut about 4cm long

200g bean sprouts

Soak the rice noodles in boiled water for 5 minutes. Drain the water immediately and run with cold water so the noodles will not turn mushy.

Heat up the cooking oil in a wok or deep frying pan. Add in the onion, garlic and ginger. Cook until the aromas rise. Add in the oyster sauce, chilli paste, soy sauce, mussels, salt, sugar and water, and cook on a medium heat until the ingredients thicken. This takes about 5 minutes. Next add in the prepared noodles, sliced onion, spring onion and green beans. Stir well to mix all the ingredients, and cook for another 5 minutes. Finally add the bean sprouts and cook until they have slightly wilted.

Ready to serve. Delicious.

Malaysians are well known for their sweet tooth. We love eating *kuih* (sweets) and normally have them for breakfast and tea time. This is something that I always miss for breakfast here in the UK. Apart from *roti canai* there is always plenty of *kuih* to choose from.

When it comes to colour and ingenuity of presentation, the variety of *kuih* demonstrates the creativity of Malaysians. Some are beautifully wrapped in banana leaves, while others are presented in unique shapes using special moulds.

I used to sell *kuih* with my brother at the local factories during their afternoon break. My Mum prepared the *kuih* and she paid us twenty cents commission for every one *ringgit kuih* sold. It was good business for all of us during school holidays!

These days most Malaysians prefer to buy *kuih* than making their own as it involves a lot of preparation. So I've chosen the easiest *kuih* recipes for you to try at home.

Buah Melaka
Glutinous Rice Balls

Makes approximately 40 balls

I love making this dessert. This is a Nyonya *dessert and some parts of Malaysia call it* onde onde. *The dough is made of glutinous rice flour and* pandan *leaf extract, filled with dark coconut sugar and coated with grated coconut. These three flavours come together into a wonderful sweet that kind of melts in your mouth as the sugar oozes out when you eat it. Nice to have after you have eaten something spicy.*

Ingredients

For the dough and filling
300g glutinous rice flour
225ml water (for the dough)
½ teaspoon salt
200g dark coconut sugar block
2 litres water (to boil)

For the coating
200g fine desiccated coconut
½ teaspoon salt

For the extract
4 *pandan* leaves
150ml water

To make the *pandan* leaf extract, cut the leaves into small pieces and put in a blender with 150ml water and blend until the leaves are ground. Squeeze the *pandan* pulp through a sieve or strainer to extract the juice. Set aside.

Cut the dark coconut sugar block into small pieces (about ¼ inch cubes). Don't worry about getting the perfect cube size as it will melt when boiled.

To make the dough, add the glutinous rice flour, 225ml water, *pandan* leaf extract and ½ teaspoon salt into a bowl and mix well to make a soft dough. To know whether the dough is well mixed and not too soft, the dough should not stick to your fingers. Form the dough into small balls about an inch in diameter. Using your thumb or fingers, gently press the dough ball flat in the middle. Place a cube of the sugar in the centre and wrap it up to make into a ball shape again. Put aside and repeat until you finish the whole dough.

Prepare the coating by placing the desiccated coconut on a flat tray. Add ½ teaspoon salt, mix in and set aside.

Here's the fun bit. Boil 2 litres water in a cooking pot. Once boiled, reduce the heat to medium and gently drop the dough balls in the boiling water. The dough balls are cooked when their colour changes and they float on the surface as the sugar cubes melt. (If you see the sugar seep through the skin that means it wasn't wrapped properly – it's still edible but will not be as sweet as one wrapped properly.) Let them float for a minute before scooping them out using a small sieve or perforated ladle.

Once scooped, drop and roll them on the bed of desiccated coconut to coat them well. Set aside for ten minutes before serving. This will help to cool down the melted sugar filling.

Cucur Kodok
Banana Fritters

Makes approximately 50 balls

The Northern part of Malaysia, near where I'm from, call these banana fritters cucur kodok. *Others call it* kuih jemput pisang. *I don't know exactly how the Northerners got the name* cucur kodok *because, if translated into English, it means toad fritter – maybe due to their size and shape. Anyway, this dessert is fairly simple to do and it works best with ripe bananas, especially when they've nearly gone black so they are sweeter. They are great for kids or a party, served with ice cream.*

Ingredients
1kg ripe bananas
4 tablespoons white sugar
12 tablespoons plain flour
6 tablespoons self raising flour
2 tablespoons water
½ teaspoon salt
1 litre cooking oil to deep fry

Peel the bananas and put them in a bowl. Mash them up until puréed. Add the sugar, plain flour, self raising flour, salt and water. Mix it well.

Heat up the cooking oil in a deep pan and, when ready, gently drop 'blobs' of the mixture into the hot oil using your fingers (only if you are confident doing it the Malaysian way). The way to do it is by scooping the mixture with your fingers and, using your thumb, gently push the mixture down so that it drops slowly into the oil. Each blob will expand to the size of a golf ball if you drop the mixture well. Alternatively you can use a spoon to drop them in.

Deep fry the balls on a medium heat until the colour changes to dark brown. Scoop them out on to kitchen paper towel to absorb excess oil.

You can serve the fritter balls on satay sticks, or just eat them straight from a bowl.

Cucur Keria

Sweet Potato Doughnut

This is a fabulous Malaysian style doughnut using sweet potato and flour. It involves quite a lot of preparation but the result, as you can see, is very good. If you are a big fan of sweet potato then you must try this recipe. The crusty sugar coating makes it look and taste scrumptious!

Ingredients

For the rings

600g sweet potato
2 litres water (to boil the potatoes)
150g plain flour
100ml water
¼ teaspoon salt
¾ litre cooking oil to deep fry

For sugar coating

300g white sugar
200ml water

Peel the sweet potatoes and cut into small pieces. Place into a deep cooking pot with the 2 litres of water and cook until the potato has gone soft. It should take about 10 to 15 minutes. Drain the water and mash the potato in the bowl. Set aside for 45 minutes to cool down.

Make sure the potato is totally cooled down before mixing it with the flour. Add 100ml of water, the salt and flour together with the mashed sweet potato. Mix it well.

Form the dough into a ring by rolling it into a log and joining both ends together to form a doughnut shape. Form each one to about 2 inches in diameter. To avoid the dough sticking to your fingers, sprinkle plain flour in your palms. Repeat the same until you finish the whole dough.

Heat up the cooking oil in a saucepan and, once hot, fry the dough rings until they have gone crispy brown. Set aside.

To prepare the sugar coating, boil 200ml of water and 300g of normal sugar in a wok or saucepan until the mixture turns into a thick syrup. Turn off the heat and add the fried dough rings into the syrup. Gently turn them and shake the pan so all the dough rings are well coated with the syrup. Quickly remove the dough rings to a plate before the syrup turns cold and crusty.

Serve them with cups of black coffee. That's how Malaysians would have them.

Ketayap
Coconut Pancake

Ketayap is a Malaysian style pancake, famously known for its green colour and aroma from pandan *leaves. The filling takes longer to prepare and can be made a day before and kept in the fridge, if you are planning ahead. The batter only takes 15 minutes to prepare. It always goes down well with my cookery school students!*

Ingredients

For the extract
8 *pandan* leaves
200ml water

For the filling
200g fine desiccated coconut
150g coconut sugar block
50g dark brown sugar
500ml water
1 *pandan* leaf (tied in a knot)

For the batter
400g plain flour
1 egg
100ml coconut milk
700ml water
¼ teaspoon salt

For frying
1 *pandan* leaf (tied in a knot)
4 tablespoons cooking oil

To make the *pandan* extract, cut the leaves into small pieces and blend in a blender with 200ml of water. Extract the juice using a sieve and discard the pulp.

The filling is made by boiling the water, coconut sugar block and dark brown sugar in a pan until the fluid is reduced to half. Next add the desiccated coconut and *pandan* leaf. Cook until the ingredients are dry and coated in the sugar.

To make the batter, add plain flour, egg, coconut milk, *pandan* leaf extract, 700ml water and salt into a bowl. Use a wooden spoon or electric hand mixer to blend the mixture.

Using a round griddle pan or shallow frying pan, grease with cooking oil using the *pandan* leaf knot. This will bring out its aroma. Using a ladle (about 60ml), make a round medium sized pancake and cook on a low heat for about 5 minutes. The bottom surface will turn slightly brown. No need to flip. Just cook one side only. Transfer the pancake to a flat surface (you can use a chopping board) and add a tablespoon or so of the sugared coconut filling across the centre of the pancake. Start folding it from the bottom up over the filling, fold in both sides and continue rolling to the top of the pancake – just like folding a spring roll.

Repeat the same until all the batter is used up. Serve warm or cold on its own, or with ice cream.

Drinks

Just like the food, Malaysian drinks are often very colourful. As well as fresh fruit juices like lychee and lime, iced drinks and sundaes are very popular as a refreshing way of washing down spicy food.

Being a Muslim country, most Malaysians do not drink alcohol, so we have lots of other interesting – and sweet – drinks instead.

My favourite is *Air Batu Campur* or ABC for short. When I tell my cookery school students about it, they are surprised to hear of the seemingly odd combination of ingredients – ice shavings, creamed sweet corn, peanuts, grass jellies, rose syrup, condensed milk and sometimes topped with ice cream – but when it melts, the flavours and textures work well together. I dare them to try it if they ever visit Malaysia.

Our tea and coffee is often sweetened with condensed milk too, which the British originally imported to Asia.

Teh Tarik
Malaysian Sweet Tea

This is Malaysians' favourite drink for breakfast and the country is well known for it. There is a massive national competition every year to find the most skilled and creative teh tarik *maker. Those who have been to Malaysia and come to my restaurant often ask for it. Teh tarik in English means pulled tea. That is how it is prepared. It's easy to get addicted to it once you get used to the sweetness of the condensed milk that is blended with the tea. For this recipe I used Malaysian 'Boh' branded tea bags which I bought in Cameron Highlands. You can replace these with normal English tea bags if you don't have any!*

Ingredients
500ml boiled water
3 tea bags
2 tablespoons white sugar
2 tablespoons condensed milk

B rew the tea bags in boiled water, as you would do normally, for about 5 minutes so it becomes quite strong. Add the sugar and condensed milk, and stir well. Take out the tea bags and, using two jugs or cafetières, pour back and forth about five or six times between the two jugs to produce a thick frothy top.

Serve it in a tall slim glass or large glass mug.

Teh Ais Lemon

Makes 2 glasses

Iced Lemon Tea

This is a very refreshing iced lemon tea which I introduced at Ning restaurant as part of our summer menu. This is slightly different from how Malaysians normally have it – which is with lime instead of lemon. I make it fusion-style by adding lemon slices and fresh mint leaves to make it even fresher. It tastes much better if the tea itself is left overnight in the fridge. Take the tea bags out if you are keeping it in the fridge, adding the lemon and mint leaves when ready to serve.

Ingredients
500ml boiled water
2 tea bags
1 lemon
2 tablespoons white sugar
6 fresh mint leaves
Ice cubes
Lemon slices and mint leaves to garnish

Add the tea bags and sugar to boiled water and set aside for an hour to cool the temperature down.

Cut the lemon into six round slices and put 3 slices in each glass. Put 3 fresh mint leaves in each glass. Crush the lemon slices and mint leaves with a wooden cocktail muddler (or you can use a wooden spoon) to squeeze the juice out of the lemon. Fill up the glass with ice cubes and pour over the cold tea. Garnish with lemon slices and mint leaves to serve.

Sirap Ros Limau
Rose Syrup with Lime

Makes 10 glasses

In Malaysia, this drink is generally served during wedding receptions. I saw my neighbour make this syrup for her daughter's wedding when I was a kid. The memory is still vivid and, amazingly, I remembered all the ingredients she put into a massive pot. I remember standing there watching her and the other neighbours cooking the syrup. The aromas of all the spices blended together with rose water makes it so special and always remind me of a Malaysian wedding. It tastes like Turkish Delight. For this recipe I add lime juice to make it really refreshing.

Ingredients

For the syrup

400ml water

400g white sugar

2 *pandan* leaves (tied in a knot)

1 star anise

1 cinnamon bark (about 5cm long)

300ml rose water

2 teaspoons red powder colouring

For the drink (per glass)

4 tablespoons syrup

1 lime wedge

200ml cold water

Ice cubes

Heat up all the syrup ingredients in a saucepan. Bring to the boil. Lower the heat and simmer until the portion has reduced to half, making syrup.

To prepare a drink, add the syrup followed by ice cubes. Squeeze the juice from the lime wedge and leave it in. The juice will create a layer for the syrup to be separated from water which looks good for presentation. Gently pour in cold water into the glass and serve with a mint leaf as garnish. Stir before drinking.

Ning
Restaurant

N ing was born out of our passion for food and hospitality. Since we were in London, Andy and I talked about setting up a restaurant but it was not until we witnessed the beginning of the regeneration of the Northern Quarter neighbourhood around us in Manchester that we started to seriously research it. Eventually it was a case of 'put up or shut up'. Being ambitious and tenacious sorts, we put up!

Established in December 2006, we began trading after gaining all the relevant permissions, backing of the bank and 4 months of designing, supervising and part fitting it out ourselves. Although I gave up my job in quantity surveying (handy for budgeting and supervising the works), Andy continued to work full time as an urban planning consultant during this time. I still don't know to this day how we did it, but we did.

Our original vision was of a friendly, independent neighbourhood restaurant with a relaxed, café-style atmosphere. We were inspired by restaurants back home in Malaysia, in Amsterdam, London, New York, Hong Kong and Bangkok. But ultimately it had to reflect our own personalities (especially mine!). I wanted it to feel contemporary and relevant to a British (Mancunian, at that) audience but with traditional Malay touches and overtones. This is reflected in our brand style and logo that my best friend Yosrie a graphic designer created, and in the traditional *batik* fabric prints around the bar, which I designed myself.

Working with the building and the bohemian, urban feel of the local area, I toiled away with my assistant Joe at chipping at plaster to reveal the original brickwork and for the first year – much to the derision of the local food critic – we kept the polished concrete floor. But it was my idea for a big feature wall, accentuated with moody uplighting, that has become the signature of our restaurant. Bedecked with exclusively-designed pink and black wallpaper, the design was inspired by our logo (which incorporates Hibiscus, the national flower

Ning at food festivals.

The Ning team and celebrity guest Mawi.

of Malaysia) and some locally designed floral wallpaper from a nearby art studio.

The reality though was not quite as pretty at the time! Not only had the buck-passing culture of the British utilities industry meant that we did not get connected to the electricity supply until three days before the official launch, but the day before the launch, the plaster was still drying. So the wallpaper could not be put up and the all the builders' kit meant that we could not clean and polish the concrete floor.

Like some reality TV show, the 12 hours before the launch were 'to the wire'. At 6am, Andy having had only half an hour's sleep on the restaurant floor, welcomed the wallpaper experts who specialised in fitting bespoke coverings and who cost as much as the design and print of them. Around them our carpenter, who had also been up all night, made the last finishing touches that he could. Wallpaper looking fantastic, our teams of staff progressively arrived, ordered into action by me – kitchen stocking, front staff training and briefing, bar stocking and so on.

Just when we thought it was all coming together, Andy was panicking! Having had to call an emergency cleaner to polish the floor, our feature centrepiece table from a nearby Danish store had still yet to arrive despite repeated reassurances the previous day that it would be delivered on time. Using his expert complaining skills, Andy persuaded the store manager that this warranted some 'extra mile' customer service, whereupon the display model was dismantled and brought to the emergent restaurant – at a negotiated discount price, of course! Time? 5pm. Start of the launch party? 6pm! Phew.

By this time, I was supervising the kitchen team preparing the complimentary party food, whilst our then Front of House Manager was doing a grand job enlisting as much help as possible to get the bar in shape. Pulling myself away to go home to refresh, Andy and I then returned, fashionably late of course. Relaxed, excited

and nervous we did not know what to expect as we wound our way through the backstreets of Manchester city centre to the restaurant. Approaching the building, the restaurant glowed with the lit-up feature wall through the large glazed shopfront and inside... touched, surprised, amazed... was heaving with people. It was happening... yes, Ning was finally happeNING!

That was a good night; our hard work paid off. But we were soon to discover that was only the beginning!

Over three years on, Ning has now firmly established itself on the Manchester restaurant scene. Our pioneering cookery school and bespoke catering service, adding a new unique touch to the culinary landscape of the city. We have hosted Malaysian Ministers, various international journalists, top Malaysian celebrity singers, Malaysian champion football teams, international corporate parties, fashion shows, weddings and engagement parties, South East Asian cultural events, British TV crews and celebrities, many loyal local customers and many other memorable people and occasions.

In 2009 I was shortlisted for Manchester's Chef of the Year and, Ning, Restaurant of the Year 2009 at the prestigious Manchester Food and Drink Festival awards. Although we were beaten to it by others who had spent millions of pounds on their restaurants, we were simply grateful for the local support and encouragement – it made our hard work feel worth it! Since then, I have had a series of TV appearances on national Malaysian and British TV and, most excitingly, have been appointed as Race Chef to the *Lotus Racing* Formula One team for the 2010 Grand Prix season!

Carlos the frog, missing in action.

Penang Island ferry and Komtar tower.

Ning
Cookery
School

W e started Malay cookery classes at Ning back in 2007, with the help of my Aunty Maziah who runs the only South East Asian performing arts group of its kind in the UK. At the time we were virtually the only restaurant in the area offering cookery classes. Nowadays you can take a cookery class in almost any cuisine you want, but we pride ourselves on being the only Malaysian cookery school in the North West of England.

Both Andy and I enjoy hosting the classes which we run at least twice a month, catering to both vegetarian and non-vegetarian tastes. As well as our regular cookery classes we also run cookery-based team building days which have proven to be very successful with local businesses as a fun and different way of engaging with their clients and colleagues.

Right from the start, my aim has been to teach local people the secrets of the Malaysian home cooking I grew up with, including classic dishes like *Rendang*, *Gulai* and *Murtabak*. It's my way of promoting the passion and diversity of my home nation. As a result, many of my students go away from the classes totally captivated and promising to visit Malaysia. I jokingly said to Andy that we should get commission from Tourism Malaysia!

Andy, who acts as the cookery school facilitator, begins each class by giving our group of students a workshop on Malaysian food culture and history with one of his engaging presentations – or 'lectures' as I tease him. As we have both spent many holidays in Malaysia we have a collection of wonderful imagery, seen throughout this book, which helps my British students experience our wonderful country – especially the food markets and typical ingredients used – from the comfort of the restaurant.

The real fun starts in the kitchen making *Murtabak*, a traditional omelette pancake, the recipe for which is on page 75. It's a great way of breaking the ice with the students, as the recipe uses a lot of familiar ingredients in a new way. I always work hard

to enable the students to be at ease with me and with each other so that everyone enjoys their experience at Ning – some enter the kitchen serious, others very chatty, some outgoing, some reserved, some are young, some older, men, women, you name it. The students love the fact that my kitchen assistants are on hand to pass the ingredients to them – it's like being on a TV cookery show!

The part of the day everyone really enjoys is making *Roti Jala* which is the traditional net-shaped pancake best served with a Malay curry or sweet chilli sauce. It's tricky for my students to master, as there is a real skill and art to it.

The really serious stuff though is making two curries. This is where Andy's introduction comes in useful. All the essential Malaysian ingredients come together in the making of *Rendang* and *Gulai* – coconut milk, lemongrass, *pandan* leaves, chillies, turmeric, ginger, galangal and various spices. I love explaining them all to my students and demonstrating the recipes in our large woks in the Ning kitchen. I do get the occasional burning of the curries, but I am always impressed with how the students master the recipes – and they often surprise themselves, lighting the kitchen with faces of delight.

By this time of course, they are all very peckish. So – if they have managed to contain themselves – we all come back together in the restaurant dining area for a meal of what we have cooked. Andy beautifully sets the table with traditional *batik* fabric cloth and the students get to eat the dishes they have created. Compliments to the chefs! It's a time for relaxing, chatting, asking any questions that have come to mind and just enjoying the exquisite Malaysian flavours – which is great, bearing in mind many of my students have not even been to my restaurant before, let alone Malaysia.

Finally, Andy presents the students with a little memento – a certificate – of their achievements and more of their food to take home.

Further information

Norman Musa

norman@ningcatering.com

www.normanmusa.com

The Ning Cookbook, recipes and links

www.malaysian-food.info

Ning Restaurant

The Burton Building

92-94 Oldham Street

Northern Quarter

Manchester

M4 1LJ

United Kingdom

+44 (0)161 238 9088

info@ningcatering.com

www.ningcatering.com

www.ningrestaurant.com

Ning Cookery School & Catering

The Burton Building

92-94 Oldham Street

Northern Quarter

Manchester

M4 1LJ

United Kingdom

+44 (0)845 519 2878

cookery@ningcatering.com

www.ningcookery.com

www.ningcatering.com

Follow us

Twitter @itsaNingthing

Become a fan of Ning

Facebook – search for Ning restaurant

Index

And Finally...

A special word of thanks to our hundreds of Cookery School students, loyal customers, friends and suppliers for making Ning possible.

Thanks also to Grace Spracklen and Andie Hall for your support at the final hurdle of preparing this book.

And a special thanks to the 'Magnet Girls', Nori, Juliana and Darlina, of MyMagneticMenu.com – for the launch of my book in Malaysia.